The Letters of the Rožmberk Sisters: Noblewomen in Fifteenth-Century Bohemia

Library of Medieval Women   **ISSN 1369–9652**

Series Editor: Jane Chance

The Library of Medieval Women aims to make available, in an English translation, significant works by, for, and about medieval women, from the age of the Church Fathers to the fifteenth century. The series encompasses many forms of writing, from poetry, visions, biography and autobiography, and letters, to sermons, treatises and encyclopedias; the subject matter is equally diverse: theology and mysticism, classical mythology, medicine and science, history, hagiography, and instructions for anchoresses. Each text is presented with an introduction setting the material in context, a guide to further reading, and an interpretive essay.

Already published

Christine de Pizan's *Letter of Othea to Hector*, *Jane Chance*, 1990

The Writings of Margaret of Oingt, Medieval Prioress and Mystic, *Renate Blumenfeld-Kosinski*, 1990

Saint Bride and her Book: Birgitta of Sweden's *Revelations*, *Julia Bolton Holloway*, 1992; new edn 2000

The Memoirs of Helene Kottanner (1439–1440), *Maya Bijvoet Williamson*, 1998

The Writings of Teresa de Cartagena, *Dayle Seidenspinner-Núñez*, 1998

Julian of Norwich: *Revelations of Divine Love* and *The Motherhood of God*, *Frances Beer*, 1998

Hrotsvit of Gandersheim: A Florilegium of her Works, *Katharina M. Wilson*, 1998

Hildegard of Bingen: *On Natural Philosophy and Medicine*: Selections from *Cause et Cure*, *Margret Berger*, 1999

Women Saints' *Lives* in Old English Prose, *Leslie A. Donovan*, 1999

Angela of Foligno's *Memorial*, *Cristina Mazzoni*, 2000

We welcome suggestions for future titles in the series. Proposals or queries may be sent directly to the editor or publisher at the addresses given below; all submissions will receive prompt and informed consideration.

Professor Jane Chance, Department of English, MS 30, Rice University, PO Box 1892, Houston, TX 77251–1892, USA. E-mail: jchance@rice.edu

Boydell & Brewer Limited, PO Box 9, Woodbridge, Suffolk, IP12 3DF, UK. E-mail: boydell@boydell.co.uk. Website: http://www.boydell.co.uk

The Letters of the Rožmberk Sisters: Noblewomen in Fifteenth-Century Bohemia

Translated from Czech and German
with Introduction, Notes and Interpretive Essay

John M. Klassen
Trinity Western University

with Eva Doležalová and Lynn Szabo

D. S. BREWER

First published 2001
D. S. Brewer, Cambridge

ISBN 0 85991 612 X

D. S. Brewer is an imprint of Boydell & Brewer Ltd
PO Box 9, Woodbridge, Suffolk IP12 3DF, UK
and of Boydell & Brewer Inc.
PO Box 41026, Rochester, NY 14604–4126, USA
website: http://www.boydell.co.uk

A catalogue record for this book is available
from the British Library

Library of Congress Cataloging-in-Publication Data
Rozmberka, Perchta z, 15th cent.
    The letters of the Rozmberk sisters: noblewomen in fifteenth-century Bohemia:
translated from Czech and German with introduction, notes and interpretive essay / John
M. Klassen, with Eva Dolezalová and Lynn Szabo.
        p. cm. – (Library of medieval women)
    ISBN 0–85991–612–X (pbk.: alk. paper)
    1. Roémberka, Perchta z, 15th cent. – Correspondence. 2. Roémberk, Anâéka, 15th
cent. – Correspondence. 3. Roémberk family. 4. Bohemia (Czech Republic) – Social life
and customs – 15th century – Sources. 5. Family life – Czech Republic – Bohemia
– History – 15th century – Sources. I. Klassen, John M. II. Dolezalová, Eva. III. Szabo, Lynn.
IV. Title. V. Series.
DB2049.R69 R69 2001
943.71'022'0922 – dc21   00–049344

This publication is printed on acid-free paper

Printed in Great Britain by
Athenæum Press Ltd, Gateshead, Tyne & Wear

Contents

Abbreviations

AČ   *Archív Český čili Staré písemné památky české a moravské* [The Czech archives or ancient written Bohemian and Moravian documents], vol. 4, ed. František Palacký (Prague: Kronberger a Řivnáč, 1844), and vol. 11, ed. Josef Kalousek (Prague: Bursík & Kohout, 1892)

Listář a listinář, 4   *Listář a listinář Oldřicha z Rožmberka 1418–1462* [Letters and Documents of Ulrich of Rožmberk 1418–1462], vol. 4, ed. Blažena Rynešová and Josef Pelikan (Prague: Státní pedagogické nakladatelství, 1954)

Sedláček, *Sborník*   Sedláček, August, 'Anéžka z Rožmberka', *Sborník Historický na oslavu desítí letého trvaní 'Klubu historického' v Praze* (Prague, 1883) [Contains the letters of Anéžka of Rožmberk]

SOA, *Cizí*   Státní Oblastní Archív in Třeboň, [The State Regional Archives in Třeboň *Z Cizí Rodi z Líchtenstejn* [Of the Foreign Family of Lichtenstejn]

Preface

The novelist Margaret Atwood suggests that the good stories about people that make up our culture,

> are about human nature, which usually means that they are about pride, envy, avarice, lust, sloth, gluttony, and anger. They are about truth and lies, and disguises and revelations; they are about crime and punishment; they are about love and forgiveness and long suffering and charity; they are about sin and retribution and sometimes even redemption.[1]

Love and forgiveness seem to have been in short supply in the life of Perchta, one of the Rožmberk sisters, but this lack is made up for in an abundance of long-suffering, avarice, truth, lies, disguises, and revelations. According to Atwood's components, Perchta's story represents a near-universal human condition. She responded to her difficult circumstances by reaching for strength within herself and for charity and redemption among her kin and friends.

The correspondence of Anéžka and Perchta of Rožmberk is significant for a number of reasons. The much more voluminous letters of Perchta illustrate how a medieval woman coped with personal unhappiness in a social system which gave her little power, teaching her to do what her father, brothers, and husband expected of her. Her letters reveal to us a woman determined to change the conditions of her bad marriage. They uncover a strategy which acknowledged the social norms founded on women's alleged inferiority. At the same time, Perchta's self-respect drove her to subvert attitudes of feminine acquiescence. She unceasingly sent letters to her father, brothers, and nephew compelling them to take note of her situation and gaining their intervention. Her letters show what a person can do in a culture in which one half of the population declares the other half as subordinate and incapable. The letters of both sisters offer insights into the hopes, joys, and vexations of fifteenth-century women. They also introduce the reader to the environment and the activities of daily castle life, ranging from

---

[1] Margaret Atwood, 'In Search of Alias Grace: On Writing Canadian Historical Fiction', *American Historical Review* 105 (1998), p. 1516.

Anéžka's pride in hunting to petty squabbles among servants. The letters also offer a detailed picture of family life in the fifteenth century. They describe the family both as a place of affection between Perchta, her father, and her siblings, but the letters also show the family to be a setting for discord and deception which the Lichtenštejn household represented for Perchta.

Perchta dictated her letters, and, as in Catherine of Siena's epistles, we get a sense of seeing oral culture on the written page.[2] Perchta was blunt, clear (except when she skipped words), passionate and articulate. Perchta's letters give the impression of a desperate breathless speaker rushing her words, changing tenses and linking together her thoughts in an itemized fashion with an abundance of ands and alsos (see for example Letter 21). Perchta's determination to get her message out despite the obstacles was clear when her secretary was absent in 1459 or early 1460. She apparently recruited a German-speaking writer and, brooking no excuses, not even ignorance of language, she pressed him into writing down her Czech words as he heard them. The misspellings are rampant, but her message comes through: life is better, but continued caution is needed to keep her dowry safe for her use (Letter 34).

The goal in translating has been to retain as much as possible of Perchta's oral dictated style while at the same time to avoid expressions awkward in English. Where words have been added to facilitate understanding they have been placed in square brackets [ ]. 'Perchta' should be pronounced, first syllable, 'pear' and *ch* as in the German *ich* or *nicht*. The *ž* is pronounced as *zh* or as in 'azure' or as the *s* in 'vision', the *š* is pronounced as *sh* in shall, and the *č* as *ch* in church.

The letters of the Rožmberk sisters are deposited in the *Státní oblastní Archív* in Třeboň, the Czech Republic, in a box labeled *Cizi Rodi z Líchtenstejn*. The translation of her Czech letters is based on the edition published by August Sedláček in *Archív Český čili staré písemné památky české í morauské* [The Czech archives or ancient written Bohemian and Moravian documents], vol. 11, ed. Josef Kalousek (Prague: Bursík & Kohout, 1892), and the original manuscripts in the archives. Her unpublished German letters are translated from the original manuscripts. The letter headings

---

2   Karen Scott, ' "*Io Catarine*": Ecclesiastical Politics and Oral Culture in the Letters of Catherine of Siena', in Karen Cherewatuk and Ulrike Wiethaus, eds., *Dear Sister: Medieval Women and the Epistolary Tradition* (Philadelphia: University of Pennsylvania Press, 1993), pp. 96, 106.

indicate the number of the letter in Sedláček's edition, as for example, *AČ* no. 1, and the word *Třeboň* in the heading indicates an unpublished letter located in the archives of Třeboň. The language of the letter is indicated just after the place of publication when known. Anéžka's letters are all in Czech and were published by August Sedláček, 'Anéžka z Rožmberka', in *Sborník Historický na oslavu desítí letého trvaní 'Klubu historického' v Praze* (Prague, 1883), and are designated in the headings by Sedláček, *Sborník*. I have followed Sedláček's spelling of Anéžka.

Money and coinage

The most reliable way to understand the value of amounts of money, such as Perchta's dowry and income, is to look at the costs and incomes of people in the fifteenth century. We know the costs of houses for Český Krumlov because in 1424, 1459 and 1466 the town authorities surveyed the citizens' wealth for purposes of taxation to defend the town. In 1459 the richest residents paid about 1700 groschen and in 1466 about 1500 groschen for their property which included a house and arable land. Artisans owning only houses paid about 348 groschen in 1459 and about 372 groschen in 1466.[3] We know little about the costs of other necessities and consumable goods in Český Krumlov but do know them for Louny, a town of comparable size in northern Bohemia. Consumer goods might vary in price considerably depending on the time of year and the available supply. In May 1470 one carp fish cost ten groschen and in March 1491 it cost six, while a tub of pike cost 160 groschen in January 1453 and 310 groschen in November 1471. From 1451 to 1461 the price of a shirt remained at about four groschen, a pair of trousers cost about six or seven groschen, a skirt, sixteen to twenty-eight groschen depending on its quality. A dress remained at about thirty groschen from 1455 to 1463. A cabinet or chest for the house cost about six groschen in the mid-1450s and a wagon of coal (*úhlí*) ranged from 44 to 114 groschen. The wagon itself cost about five or six groschen, unless it was built for a lord, in which case it cost 160 groschen. The cost of war horses ranged from 240 groschen to a high of 1140

[3] Anděla Fialová and Josef Hejnice, 'Český Krumlov v době Husitské' [Český Krumlov during the Hussite Period], in *Acta Musei Nationalis Pragae*, Series A – *Historia*, Vol. 29 (1975), no. 1, p. 14.

groschen.[4] In terms of income, a skilled artisan in Prague or a mercenary soldier received one groschen a day as wage or living allowance. The richest of the lesser nobles had a family income of about 2000 groschen a year. The letter-writers used two currencies, the Prague groschen and the Hungarian gulden. From 1459 to 1465 the number of groschen per Hungarian gulden ranged from a low of 34 up to 48.[5]

In translating the correspondence I have received substantial assistance from Eva Doležalová, of the Historical Institute in Prague, and Lynn Szabo, of Trinity Western University. It gives me considerable pleasure to thank them both for their work. Ms. Doležalová's knowledge of fifteenth-century Czech history and language, especially its idioms, has been invaluable in avoiding mistakes in translating Perchta's Czech letters. Ms. Szabo read over my translations and helped turn them into smooth readable English. In addition I would like to thank Dr. Miloslav Polívka of the Historical Institute in Prague for his assistance in preparing Perchta's German letters. I am grateful to Jennifer Hamel for helping with the proof-reading. I especially want to express my gratitude to Professor Jane Chance of Rice University, editor of this series, to Caroline Palmer of Boydell & Brewer Ltd, and to Miss Linda Gowans. All three made numerous suggestions for making this volume more accessible and useful. I want to thank the Canadian people for providing funding for this project through The Social Science and Research Council of Canada.

John M. Klassen
June 2000
Fort Langley, British Columbia

---

[4]   Jaroslav Vaniš, 'Ceny v Lounech v druhé polovině 15. století' [Prices in Louny in the second half of the fifteenth century], *Economic History* 8 (1981), pp. 5–84. For the gentry, see Miloslav Polívka, 'A Contribution to the Problem of Property Differentiation of the Lesser Nobility in the Pre-Hussite Period in Bohemia', *Economic History* 2 (1978), pp. 331–59.

[5]   Vincent Brandl, *Glossarium illustrans bohemico-moravicae historiae fontes* (Brno: Nakladatelství Carl Winiker, 1876), p. 52.

Introduction
The Rožmberk Family in Fifteenth-Century Bohemia

The home of the Rožmberk family was a realm of politics, economics, and culture, as well as a space for nurturing of personal and social bonds between brothers and sister. The correspondence of Perchta and Anéžka reveals not only two self-assured sisters, but a strong family of a father and children whose mother died while they were young. The siblings shared domestic space as they grew up under the supervision of a politically involved father to whom they were free to express affection and their most intimate secrets, before whom they could bring their anger and disappointments as well as their hopes and joys. Their home fostered individual confidence as well as a spirit of sibling solidarity. Family bonds remained strong when they as adults rallied to support their sister, Perchta, who was confronted by the strains of personal suffering and loneliness.

1. Daughters of Power

The Rožmberk sisters were members of the most powerful noble family in late medieval Bohemia. Resident in south Bohemia, the Rožmberks were the most successful branch of the Vitkovec family, which traced its origins to Vitek I (d. 1194), who acquired vast expanses of wooded lands, taking advantage of inter-family squabbles in the ruling family. The Vitkovec line skilfully used marriage strategies to increase its holdings, and Rožmberk women, such as Perchta's grandmother who helped arrange her daughter's marriage, were well aware of their importance as brides in the family's pursuit of success and status.[1]

Sometime before 1250 the Rožmberks built a large castle on the upper Vltava River, and according to the knightly fashion of the day, gave it a German name, Rosenberg, after their emblem the rose, but used its Czech form, Rožmberk. Rožmberk ambitions and sense of importance were further reflected in the building of a grandiose

---

[1] *Listář a listinář Oldřicha z Rožmberka 1418–1462* [Letters and Documents of Ulrich of Rožmberk 1418–1462], vol. 1, ed. Blažena Rynešová (Prague: Státní Tiskárna, 1929), p. 1.

Cistercian monastery at Vyšší Brod in 1259, which became not only an ecclesiastical administrative centre but also the burial place for the family. Early in the fourteenth century the Rožmberks inherited Český Krumlov from a related line which had become extinct, and it became the main family residence which they turned into a princely center of culture. By the time Perchta's father, Ulrich (1403–62), came of age in 1418, the Rožmberk estate consisted of some twenty-two castles, six towns, and almost 500 villages.[2] The family dominated the south and influenced Bohemian politics well into the sixteenth century.

Anéžka and Perchta were born during the last years of the Hussite revolution, which shook the traditional political and religious structures of medieval Bohemia. The Rožmberks had always played an important part in the politics of Bohemia, and in the fifteenth century Ulrich of Rožmberk, their father, was expected to take a leading place in defending the old order. For generations Rožmberks held a significant position in the supreme council of the central government in Prague and filled the position of regional justice for south Bohemia. They were able to play a decisive role in their country's politics not because they owed their power to royal favor but because of their extensive land holdings. As long as the rulers respected their local autonomy, the Rožmberks were prepared to support the central government. Ulrich's father, Henry (d. 1412), played a key role in the late fourteenth and early fifteenth centuries in stopping King Wenceslas' efforts to weaken the nobility and increase the monarchy's status and power.[3] Perchta's father, Ulrich, assumed control of the Rožmberk estates in 1418, from his guardian Čeněk of Vartenberk, just as the Hussite revolution broke out.

---

[2] The pre-fifteenth-century history is drawn from Jaroslav Pánek, *Poslední Rožmberkové velmozí české Renasance* [The Last Rožmberks, Magnates of the Czech Renaissance] (Prague: Panorama, 1989), pp. 21–6; Ivana Raková, 'Rožmberské teritorium v předvečer husitské revoluce' [Rožmberk Landholdings on the Eve of the Hussite Revolution], *Folia Historica Bohemica* 3 (1981); František Šmahel et al., *Dějiny Tábora* [The History of Tabor] (Česká Budějovice: Jihočeské nakladatelství, 1988–90), pp. 95–99, 142–43; and Robert Šimůnek, 'Dědictví po Čeněk z Vartenberka (Krožmbersko-vartenberským vztahu v 1. polovině 15. století)' [The Estate of Čeněk of Vartenberk (On Rožmberk-Vartenberk Relations in the first half of the fifteenth Century)], *Mediaevalia Historica Bohemia* 5 (1998), pp. 103–16.

[3] John M. Klassen, *The Nobility and the Making of the Hussite Revolution*, East European Monographs, vol. 47 (New York: Columbia University Press, 1978), pp. 5–18.

The Hussites were followers of John Hus, whom a Church Council of prominent clergy, meeting in Constance, condemned to be burned at the stake in 1415. Hus had inspired his countrymen and women with his vision of a reformed Church and to stand up for themselves as members of the Czech people. He was critical of the clergy for its wealth and use of secular power and he encouraged both women and men to actively pursue the moral reform of the Church and its members. Hus was concerned for the welfare of the poor, for wholesome sexual morals, and encouraged women to think of themselves as created in the image of God. After his death, the Hussites introduced the practice of taking wine in the Eucharist and adopted the chalice as their symbol. The revolution of his supporters did not actually break out until 1419 after King Sigismund claimed the Czech crown and initiated a campaign to suppress the Hussites. The revolution split Bohemia into three parts: the radical Hussites, called Taborites, the moderates, and those loyal to the Catholic church.[4]

In the first phase of the revolution the radicals, consisting largely of commoners, threatened to abolish the whole medieval structure of government headed by nobles and king. They chose a deserted fortress on the northern fringes of the Rožmberk domains, which they named Tabor and developed into the main center of revolutionary activity. In 1420 they captured a number of important Rožmberk castles, which served as their first line of defence. Consequently, Ulrich's earliest efforts had to be directed at safeguarding his estates from the Taborite radicals of the revolution, while the Catholics and royalists also looked to him to provide national leadership.

Perchta's fate was to some extent caught up in Bohemian partisan strife, but her father did not entirely allow the needs of the kingdom to distract him from his family's needs. By the 1430s, he had reached an arrangement with his radical neighbors, the Taborites, so that both could live in relative peace. His political troubles originated from the more moderate Hussite nobles. The political divisions in Bohemia mainly followed religious lines, although a person's stance could be motivated by a wide array of forces. The Catholics tended to favor the Austrian succession, while the Hussites favored a Polish or Czech king, although there were people

---

[4] See Howard Kaminsky, *A History of the Hussite Revolution* (Berkeley: University of California Press, 1967), and John Klassen, *Warring Maidens, Captive Wives and Hussite Queens*, East European Monographs, vol. 527 (New York: Columbia University Press, 1999), pp. 162–67, for Hus's views on gender.

who crossed over the confessional line. The deaths in quick sequence of King Sigismund in 1437 and of his heir Albrecht of Austria in 1439 meant an uncertain succession for the Czech monarchy and years of political unrest. Perchta's father was the undisputed leader of the Catholic–Austrian party and the uncertain state of affairs required his attention, especially after King Albrecht's death.[5]

Perchta's dowry was slow in coming, partly because the political situation after 1440 did not develop well for her father. Ulrich of Rožmberk started out strongly when in 1439 he led the Czech nobility in the festive procession which welcomed Albrecht of Austria as king. Albrecht rewarded Ulrich by making him the supreme burgrave of the land, the official next in power to the king. But Ulrich was unable to take good advantage of the ensuing uncertainties. In 1445 he protected the unpopular papal representative, John Carvajel, who refused to confirm King Sigismund's charter of 1436, the so-called Compacts, which promised the Czechs the right to take wine in communion. Carvajel added to the people's wrath when he tried to steal the original copy of the Charter. In the meantime Rožmberk's rival, George of Poděbrady, the leader of the Hussite–Polish party, steadily increased his appeal by cooperating with Ladislas, the child-king, who died in 1457, a ward of Frederick III of Austria. In 1448 Poděbrady took Prague by force and replaced an administration loyal to Rožmberk's Catholic–Austrian party with his own supporters.[6] These setbacks meant that Ulrich had to place more energy and resources into diplomatic and military activity in order to regain his position. Despite the need to recover his influence, Ulrich did not ignore his daughter. On 20 October 1449 he writes a fellow nobleman that for the next several weeks he will be preoccupied 'with feasting and the wedding which I will have soon at the giving away of my daughter, which is no secret to you'.[7] Rožmberk's greatest defeat came in March 1458 when the Czech estates elected his rival, George of Poděbrady, as king. The coronation of Poděbrady was especially stinging to Rožmberk because his son John, in exchange for cancelling a debt and thus freeing funds

---

[5] Šmahel, *Dějiny*, pp. 523–31.
[6] Šmahel, *Dějiny*, pp. 531–42, and Václav V. Tomek, *Dějepis Města Prahy* [A History of the City of Prague], 6 (Prague: Fr. Řivnáče, 1906), pp. 114, 145–55, 186.
[7] *Listář a listinář*, 4, p. 114. See also Miloslav Polívka, 'Ulrich von Rosenberg und seine Umgebung', in *Adelige Welt und familiäre Beziehung*, ed. Heinz-Dieter Heimann (Potsdam: Verlag für Berlin-Brandenburg, 2000), pp. 67–68, n. 42.

for Perchta's dowry, cast his vote on behalf of Poděbrady. His action reversed decades of family politics closely tied to the Roman Church and aimed at developing contacts and support in Austria.

Ulrich of Rožmberk's financial difficulties, which were the indirect cause of Perchta's predicament, stemmed from a variety of sources. By the time of Perchta's marriage in November 1449, Rožmberk's incomes from his lands had recovered from the losses of the Hussite revolution.[8] In the meantime, however, diplomatic, military, and cultural expenses took up increasing shares of income, resulting in huge debts by the end of his life.

Rožmberk decided to delay Perchta's dowry, preferring to use funds on diplomatic and military activities which would shore up his influence and authority and to pursue a far-reaching policy to consolidate his lands and diversify the output of his estates. His willingness to go into debt limited the scope of his and his sons' activities in the second part of the fifteenth century, but his action bore fruit for his heirs in the sixteenth century. Subsequent Rožmberk lords profited from the growing demand for food not only in Bohemia but in the Alpine region in general.[9] His daughter's dowry also took second place to Rožmberk's ambition to turn Český Krumlov into a significant center of Czech medieval culture. In the years before her wedding, from 1444 to 1447, Rožmberk had his upper castle rebuilt into a spacious three-winged residence. When the Hussite revolution drove many of Europe's intellectuals and artists out of Prague, some of them found refuge in Český Krumlov, which in many ways replaced Prague as the center of Czech culture.[10] Some came to stay, whereas others, such as Aeneas Sylvius Piccolomini and John Capistrano, came for short visits to the home of the baron who was central to the church of Rome's campaign to free Bohemia of the Hussite religion. Their presence meant increased economic activity but, as their patron, Rožmberk felt obligated to pay their expenses, so that fewer funds were available for Perchta's dowry. Rožmberk's economic, political, and military priorities contributed to Perchta's powerlessness during the

---

8 Šmahel, *Dějiny*, 2, pp. 345–50. For the date of Perchta's wedding, see Anna Kubíková, 'Rožmberské kroniky krátky a summovní výtah VII. kapitoly – Oldřich II. z Rožmberka' [The Short Rožmberk Chronicles and Summary Extract Chapter 7 – Ulrich II of Rožmberk], *Jihočeský sborník historický* 58 (1989), p. 204.

9 Pánek, *Poslední*, pp. 23, 25–26.

10 For the following see Anna Skýbová, *Listy Bílé Paní Rožmberské* [Letters of the White Lady Rožmberk] (Prague: Panorama, 1985), pp. 12–13.

first years of her marriage. By delaying the dowry, her father sacrificed her well-being for his lineage's later prosperity and glory.

When Rožmberk delayed sending Perchta's dowry, he most probably believed he had a period of grace within which to fulfil his promise and that her husband would not leave her penniless. Non-delivery of the marriage gift was not rare among his peers, the nobility of the Holy Roman Empire. The problem in Germany was so widespread that some husbands reserved the right to return the bride to her family if she did not present the dowry at the agreed-upon time.[11] Despite the risk, heads of families sometimes delayed remitting the gift for years, if not decades, so in Rožmberk's mind his daughter would probably not suffer exceptionally adverse consequences if he delayed provision of the dowry.

2. Growing up in the Rožmberk household

Perchta and Anéžka grew up without a mother, but with a caring father, who, in the midst of his political, military, and economic activities, gave them his attention. Their mother, Catherine, died in 1436 when Perchta was seven years old. Neither Anéžka nor Perchta mentions either mother or a step-mother in her letters. Catherine had six children, Perchta (d. 2 May 1476), Anéžka (d. 25 July 1488), Lidmila (d. unknown), Henry (d. 1457), John (d. 8 February 1472) and Jošt (d. 12 December, 1467). When Catherine died, supervising the children's upbringing fell to Ulrich.

3. Education and training

The education of a daughter was an important investment for European aristocrats and royalty, requiring considerable attention.[12] A father who ignored his daughter's training was in dereliction of duty, neglecting a valuable resource who in her new home was positioned fundamentally to effect the fortunes of her family of birth. As potential marriage candidates, the daughters required abilities and knowledge which would determine their success. As wives in families whose friendship the marriage was designed to strengthen, they had to know how to behave, and they needed to know something about bridge-building, about diplomacy, and about ritual. We have

---

[11] Karl-Heinz Spieß, *Familie und Verwandschaft im deutschen Hochadel des Spätmittelalters* (Stuttgart: Steiner Verlag, 1993), pp. 167–72.

[12] John C. Parsons, 'Mothers, Daughters, Marriage, Power: Some Plantagenet Evidence 1150–1500', in *Medieval Queenship*, ed. John C. Parsons (New York: St. Martin's Press, 1993), pp. 63–78.

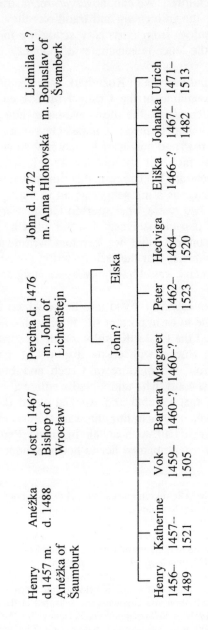

Children and grandchildren of
Ulrich of Rožmberk d. 1462 and Catherine of Vartenberk d. 1436
married in 1418

Henry
d.1457 m.
Anéžka of
Šaumburk

Anéžka
d. 1488

Jost d. 1467
Bishop of
Wrocław

Perchta d. 1476
m. John of
Lichtenštejn

John d. 1472
m. Anna Hlohovská

Lidmila d. ?
m. Bohuslav of
Švamberk

John?   Elska

Henry
1456–
1489

Katherine
1457–
1521

Vok
1459–
1505

Barbara
1460–?

Margaret
1460–?

Peter
1462–
1523

Hedviga
1464–
1520

Eliška
1466–?

Johanka
1467–
1482

Ulrich
1471–
1513

little direct knowledge about the upbringing experienced by the Rožmberk children. We can, however, reconstruct with a fair degree of certainty the influences and traditions they were exposed to in Český Krumlov, from university schooling to economic developments and the legends and fables of popular culture and of saints' lives.

Anéžka and Perchta of Rožmberk participated in the learning and education available in the Český Krumlov castle. The Rožmberk sons had access to the best available education in Bohemia, including teachers trained at Charles University in Prague.[13] Perchta was able to read and may have known how to write in her own hand, although the fact that she did not herself write when her Czech-speaking secretary left suggests that this may not have been the case. Urgencies such as a messenger about to leave, or writing in secret from one's bed, were what spurred German aristocratic women to take up the pen themselves.[14] On the other hand, Perchta may not have been confident that her own handwriting would be legible, or she may have felt that the task of writing was beneath her dignity when a secretary was at hand, just as washing her own dresses might have been.

Perchta and Anéžka lived in a home which Ulrich of Rožmberk had made the most important site for Czech culture next to Prague. He decorated the Český Krumlov castle in splendor and welcomed guests from abroad with costly displays of magnificence. Perchta benefited from the mixture of Czech and European intellectuals present at his court, who undoubtedly enlarged her perspectives. It is most likely that Perchta and Anéžka heard their brothers discuss events in Bohemia including the wars (Letter 49) and the land diets or parliaments.[15] In such an environment Perchta and the young women who accompanied her to her new home learned the impor-

---

[13] Josef Hejnic, 'Českokrumlovská latinská škola v době rožmberské' [The Latin School in Český Krumlov during the Time of the Rožmberks], *Rozpravy Československé Akademie Věd* (Prague: 1972).

[14] See Cordula Nolte, *'Pey eytler finster in einem weichen pet geschrieben*. Eigenhändige Briefe in der Familienkorrespondenz der Markgrafen von Brandenburg (1470–1530)', in *Adelige Welt*, ed. Heimann, pp. 177–202, and her unpublished paper, 'Überlegungen zu eigenhandigen Familienbriefen: Die Korrespondenz Amilies von Pfalz-Zweibrucken-Veldenz mit ihren Eltern, Kurfurst Albrecht Achilles und Anna von Bradenburg', delivered at the Conference *Die private Welt des Adels in Selbstzeugnissen*, Potsdam, 22–25 October 1997. I wish to thank the author for providing me with a copy of her paper.

[15] Skýbová, *Listy*, p. 21.

tance of writing and the role of letters, and became acquainted with epistolary forms. In Český Krumlov castle Perchta learned the standards of feminine behavior of the noble class of that time and the practical knowledge needed to run a household, such as basic arithmetic, including addition and subtraction, as well as her property and financial rights (Letters 38 and 67). Here also family members discussed ways to diversify the estate's sources of income. From such discussions grew Anéžka's interest in different breeds of cattle (Letter 70) and the family decision to expand fish production by promoting a system of fish ponds.

The most important part of Perchta's education was that as a wife she had to obey and submit to her husband, her new lord. Her training resembled that of young noblewomen throughout Europe who heard or read the teachings of preachers and other moralists, as well as values transmitted by courtly literature. We can be reasonably sure that the principles that Perchta learned in the Rožmberk household resembled the Czech religious teaching on domesticity as presented by a member of the gentry, Thomas of Štítný, a layman and a widower with two children, active in Prague early in the fifteenth century. His lessons on male privilege are contained in his tract, *On the Master, the Mistress, and the Children,*[16] where Štítný described the father as the master who represented the sun. From him the mother, as the moon, and the children, as the stars, received their light. The father led by example and by command and the other members of his household obeyed. Štítný wrote that a wife must not forget that her glory came from her husband and she should not give herself airs about how important her family was. Nor should she use the property she brought into the union, or her intelligence, as a means to impress and manipulate her husband. A wife did have legitimate rights and authority within Štítný's patriarchal hierarchy. Ideally she could expect love, gratitude, service, forbearance, and diligence from her husband, which she was to return to him. Štítný's advice to a wife whose husband did not love her was to return kindness for his dislike; he promised that she would thus eventually win his love. Perchta knew that if her husband persisted in his malice

---

[16] Tomaš Štítný. *Knížky o hře šachové a jiné* [Thomas Štítný. Books about the Game of Chess and other things], ed. František Šimek, and Miloslav Kaňak, (Prague: Státní Nakladatelství Krásné Literatury, Hudby a Umění, 1956), pp. 99–109. See also Anna Šubrtová, 'Populační myšlení v české homiletice feudálního období' [Popular Notions in Czech Sermons of the Middle Ages], *Časopis Národního Muzea – řada historiká* 157 (1988), p. 119.

and ill will, she should continue in her obedience because she would have her reward from God (Letter 39 PS).

Perchta and Anéžka's learning in feminine submissiveness also reflected what their father and brothers understood as their rights as lords. A nobleman believed that his wife owed him obedience by virtue of his right as lord. The jurist Kornel of Všehrd pointed out that a husband could do with his wife almost anything he wanted to. In practice, Kornel writes, 'Wives are captives of their husbands, because they have to do everything their husbands order them to do, just as captives have to do what those who have captured and overcome them, order them to do.'[17] As a child Perchta saw a father who modelled both authority and consideration. Ulrich of Rožmberk maintained the view that a lord and husband had the right to lock up a dangerous wife. He expressed this opinion when he heard of the case in 1446 of a nobleman, Zdeněk of Šternberk, whose wife had been implicated in a plot to poison him. Zdeněk refused to sleep with her, but otherwise allowed her to walk about freely. Rožmberk showed surprise at his peer's patience with his independent-minded and dangerous wife.[18] Perchta's frequent assertions of obedience to her husband indicate her father's values had been heard.

Perchta also saw a more sensitive side of her father. Although it is rare to have a medieval nobleman express feelings for his wife, there is evidence that his wife Catherine's final sickness kept Ulrich at her bedside. A letter from Queen Barbara in June 1436, just after Catherine's death, expressing her sympathy with his loss, suggests that his wife's state of health was responsible for Ulrich's absence from attending two significant political ceremonial occasions in Jihlava, Moravia. During her mother Catherine's last illness in the spring of 1436, Perchta's father did not travel to Jihlava for the formal celebration and signing of the conclusive peace accord between Emperor Sigismund and his Czech subjects, and his long-delayed public recognition as King of Bohemia, despite strong pressure from the emperor and his wife Barbara to do so.[19] Perchta knew that she herself was important to her father when in the autumn of 1449

---

[17] M. *Viktorina ze Všehrd O právích země české* (Master Viktorine of Všehrd, About the Laws of the Czech Land), ed. Hermenegild Jireček (Prague: Všehrd, 1874), p. 228.

[18] *AČ*, 4, pp. 9–10. Compare Joel. T. Rosenthal, 'Aristocratic Marriage and the English Peerage, 1350–1500: Social Institution and Personal Bond', *Journal of Medieval History* 10 (1984), pp. 181–83, 186.

[19] *Listář a listinář* 1, p. 202, and Kubiková, *Rožmberské kroniky*, p. 147.

Rožmberk chose to stay home to prepare for her wedding instead of attending a Land diet where his peers discussed policies and actions designed to undermine Ulrich's rival, George of Poděbrady. Ulrich's desire to be with his wife in her time of need, and to help his daughter celebrate, prevailed over his political and diplomatic responsibilities.

It is evident from Perchta's words that she expected something like the courtly game of love between lady and lover, and the social and physical intimacy as described by the French husband in the *Ménagier de Paris*. He encouraged his wife to soothe her husband's body and let him rest his head between her breasts. If treated well, he wrote, the husband will feel for his wife what a child feels for those who love it.[20] In a rare happy moment Perchta writes, 'thanks be to God, I have what I need to eat and to drink, and my husband eats with me and has been with me since the time that I arranged and organized those affairs [for him]' (Letter 39; see also Letter 34). Her joy was short-lived and her marriage continued to be disappointing because her husband had no interest in the physical intimacy described by courtly poets and by the Parisian husband (Letters 13 and 15).

Perchta's moral and religious education taught her the importance of wifely obedience, but she also learned that she could expect authority and honor in her home. Writers from Christine de Pizan to Thomas of Štítný described the wife as the ruler, the person after her husband on the ladder of the domestic hierarchy. She ran the household, hired the household staff, gave orders to children and servants, planned meals and banquets, and made numerous daily decisions which required access to necessary funds. It was her responsibility to mediate disputes among the servants, to raise the children, and generally to keep household peace.[21] Without the loyalty of the castle servants and retinue a wife was in no position to assure

---

[20] Georges Duby, 'The Courtly Model', in *A History of Women in the West*, II, *Silences of the Middle Ages*, ed. Christiane Klapisch-Zuber (Cambridge MA: Harvard University Press, 1992), pp. 254–55; Emilie Amt, ed., *Women's Lives in Medieval Europe* (New York: Routledge, 1993), p. 321; and D. Régnier-Bohler, 'Imagining the Self – Exploring Literature', *History of Private Life*: vol. II, *Revelations of the Medieval World*, ed. George Duby (Boston: Harvard University Press, 1988), p. 350.

[21] Štítný, *Knížky*, p. 108, For Christine, see Amt, *Women's Lives*, pp. 323–30. See also Heidi Wunder, *He is the Sun, She is the Moon Women in Early Modern Germany* (Cambridge MA: Harvard University Press, 1998), 156–60, and Spieß, *Familie*, pp. 147–48.

orderly administration. It is clear from her letters that her powerlessness in the face of her mother-in-law's authority was the most distressing aspect of her married life (Letters 7 and 26).

The Rožmberk household's concern for things Czech and for religion meant that the children were likely well-steeped in native folklore and in the lives of the saints. Popular stories and fantasies provided a script for women's behavior which undermined passivity and submission as an ideal by depicting some famous Czech women as wise and assertive. This is especially true of the foundation legends.[22] One of the more popular traditions told the story of Libuše, the first ruler of the Czechs, and the warring maidens. An anonymous nobleman who recorded the legend in the early fourteenth century called her the mother of the land, whose wise rule was foolishly challenged by men on the basis of her sex. Libuše gave up her rule and when she died a group of women led by Vlasta, Šarka, and others, went to war against the men. The warring women enjoyed considerable popularity and admiration in the later memory of the Czech people. In addition, the Rožmberk library contained a copy of the Czech *Life of Saint Catherine*,[23] and Catherine's example of courage and resilience in the face of torture and hardships may well have inspired Perchta to persevere. Perchta, however, had no taste for martyrdom, and acted resolutely to improve the material circumstances of her life.

Respect for Libuše was apparent among story-tellers of the common people, who told of ghostly female figures appearing to people in need and doing kindly deeds. The populace in south Bohemia gave the names of Libuše, Vlasta, and Šarka to these benevolent apparitions in honor of their illustrious foremothers. In the late 1440s, during the contested election for the throne, Libuše's warning against foreign rulers was reaffirmed by those supporting the native candidate, George of Poděbrady. The late fifteenth-century jurist, Kornel of Všehrd, extended his tribute not only to Libuše, but to the other ancestral women, elevating their military expertise in his introduction to Czech law. The patriotic legends of Libuše and Vlasta fit in well in the Rožmberk home with its pride in Czech culture. These stories of proud and able women from their past helped produce notions of gender behavior among girls and

---

[22] See Klassen, *Warring Maidens*, pp. 14–29.

[23] Alfred Thomas, *Anne's Bohemia: Czech Literature and Society, 1310–1420* (Minneapolis MN: University of Minnesota Press, 1998), pp. 88–109.

young women, encouraging them to believe in their dignity and strength.

4. Perchta's siblings

The early death of his wife Catherine meant that Ulrich took on the responsibility of raising the children, even if not directly and personally. Ulrich's correspondence with a wide range of people, from his children to kings and emperors, reflects his ability to establish an atmosphere of openness in his family. He showed no shame or embarrassment when sharing sensitive matters such as his own illness and inter-family quarrels. He expressed his commitment to cooperative relations and his faith in his sons when in November 1451 he made all three of them full partners with him in administering the estates.[24] His children knew that they could contact him without fear of rebuff. The term of address from his eldest daughter Anéžka, 'my daddy', reflected her feeling of intimacy and trust towards her father (Letter 22). Because she had found him at hand as a child, Perchta, as a lonely wife, knew that she could freely write to her father about her problems in a hostile new home.

Of the six children, Lidmila is the least well known. She survived into adulthood, married Bohuslav of Švamberk in 1451, and apparently lived without the problems in her marriage that Perchta experienced. Her dowry estate was Bor in western Bohemia. Later, she and her husband moved to her Rožmberk family's castle, Zvíkov, and then to Český Krumlov when her husband was appointed the governor of the Rožmberk lands. She had at least one son, described as good-looking and brave in battle. Lidmila predeceased her husband and we know nothing else about her.[25]

Perchta's brothers were her closest and most effective allies and friends. As Rožmberk sons, they too exercised power and influence in Bohemia's political life and were in a position to help their sister. Recently, Anna Skýbová described Perchta's oldest brother, Henry, as the political type and a hardened warrior, and most like his father. He served in the army of Emperor Frederick III from 1447 to 1449,

---

[24] *AČ*, 11, p. 258.
[25] Rudolf Urbánek, 'Dvě Rožmberkovny, Anežka a Perchta' [Two Rožmberk Women, Anéžka and Perchta], *Královny, Kněžny a velké Ženy České* [Queens, Princesses and Great Czech Women], ed. Karel Stloukal (Prague: J. R. Vilímek, 1940), p. 188, Sedláček, *Sborník*, p. 111, and August Sedláček, *Hrady, Zámky a Tvrze České* [Czech Castles, Palaces and Fortresses], vol. 13 (Prague: Šolc a Šimáček, 1936), pp. 45–46, 109.

engaged in jousts with Albert the margrave of Brandenberg, and responded to King Ladislas' invitation to aid Belgrade against the Turks in 1456. On his way home he fell ill and died in Vienna in January 1457.[26] Perchta and Anéžka were both close to him, and while still at home, sometime in the 1440s, eagerly expressed their anticipation over his return from service in the emperor's army, at the forthcoming carnival time (Letter 1). In July 1450, when he asked her to stop writing and keep the peace, Perchta astutely informed him that through his influence she had the courage to act on her own behalf; what she was doing she had learned from him. In a personal touch she sent him a shirt which she asked him to wear. In 1455, her father entrusted Henry to meet Perchta in Vienna, care for her, and speak on her behalf in negotiations with Lichtenštejn.

Ulrich of Rožmberk designated his son Jošt for the clergy. Jošt was well educated, knowing Latin, Italian, and German. Since the Hussite revolution had emaciated the Catholic church in Bohemia, Jošt found the fulfilment of his career aspirations in another land of the Czech crown, nearby Silesia, becoming the Bishop of Wrocław. His German-speaking parishioners censured him because his mastery of their language was not up to their standards, as well as for his love of food and of beautiful women. He remained involved in both Bohemian politics and the life of his family. In 1461, in a mediation finding of a quarrel between his brother John and his father, Jošt ordered that first of all his brother and father should banish 'all dislike, fighting, anger, bad will, and unfriendly thoughts from their hearts'.[27] Perchta included Jošt in her correspondence, in late 1463, informing him (Letter 39) about her husband's questionable money decisions and her own efforts to raise money to rescue him. She made Jošt her heir to the bond, and requested his and her brother John's counsel in her decision to leave her husband. She ended her letter with a request on behalf of both her husband and herself that he send a first-class coat made of marten furs.

Perchta's relationship to her youngest brother, John, was the most crucial in her efforts to gain security and independence. According to Anna Skýbová he was the best educated and the most tolerant of the Rožmberk men.[28] He seems to have been a favorite for both Anéžka and Perchta. Perchta expressed a personal tenderness

---

[26] Kubíková, *Rožmberské kroniky*, pp. 202–203.
[27] *Listář a listinář*, 4, p. 444.
[28] Skýbová, *Listy*, 18.

towards him, as he did to her. In 1460 she wrote to him of her great joy at the reconciliation with her husband and asked him to give his seal of approval by sending her husband some trout (Letter 34). In 1463 he expressed his great sorrow at learning that she was again poor and unhappy. In thanking her for a scarf she had sent, he wrote that he did so as he would thank a lover (Letter 41).

Perchta's and John's mutual regard helped bring about a decisive change in Rožmberk politics, which facilitated the payment of the dowry for which Perchta had waited for close to ten years. Despite massive debts, which Skýbová estimated to be around 1,000,000 groschen by 1462, John and his father had choices as to where to invest their money. A complete study of Rožmberk incomes has not been conducted, but it is known that even in bad years the Rožmberks had sufficient income to allow an element of choice in their decision-making. During the years of the revolution, the peasants on Bechyň estate alone brought the Rožmberks a half-year's income of 23,800 groschen.[29] By the mid-1450s, with the 60,000-groschen dowry still undelivered, the Rožmberks began to use some of their income for Perchta and made the twice-annual payment of 3,000 groschen to Lichtenštejn agreed to in the marriage contract. According to the contract, with the dowry delivered she was to get 15,000 groschen a year (Letter 2). The full dowry was not paid until 1460 after John of Rožmberk paid off one of his estate's large debts by giving his support to George of Poděbrady, the leader of the opposing Hussite faction.

Among his liabilities, Ulrich owed the Austrian duke Frederick of Etsse some 16,000 gulden, equivalent to about 544,000 groschen.[30] When Frederick sold the promissory note to George of Poděbrady, the Rožmberks owed this huge amount to their political rival. It seems John wanted to make an arrangement with Poděbrady but his father Ulrich disagreed sharply with his son, so they submitted their quarrel to mediation. In January 1458 the mediators issued their finding ordering the father Ulrich to give up to his son John his copy of the promissory note describing the Poděbrady debt. The mediators inserted a clause reflecting Ulrich's concern for his estates. John was

---

[29] Skýbová, *Listy*, p. 16. For Rožmberk incomes, see Šmahel, *Dějiny Tábora*, p. 350.

[30] During 1459–1465 the number of groschen per Hungarian gulden ranged from a low of 34 up to 48. Vincent Brandl, *Glossarium illustrans bohemico-moravicae historiae fontes* (Brno: Nakladatelství Carl Winiker, 1876), p. 52. See the Preface, p. ix, for a fuller discussion of money values.

instructed to resolve the debt to Poděbrady, but in terms that brought no harm to the Rožmberk estates.[31] In early 1458, in the midst of political manoeuvring and electioneering for the Czech throne, John of Rožmberk agreed to support his father's rival George of Poděbrady in exchange for the latter's canceling the 544,000 groschen owing. After the elections, John of Rožmberk continued to show his support for Poděbrady by accompanying the new king on the celebratory procession through Prague.[32] Freed from this large liability, John set about helping his sister. Ten years after Perchta's wedding, in 1460, he promised to deliver the full amount, 60,000 groschen, of his family's marriage gift before the end of the year. In an undated letter in 1460, Perchta wrote to her brother John indicating how to time the delivery of the dowry, which she knew was now coming. She ends the letter 'I often wrote with great sorrow, but this letter with great joy' (Letter 34). Lichtenštejn issued a receipt for 28,800 groschen to Rožmberk, dated 4 February 1460. Although no receipt for the remainder survives, presumably it too was paid.

Rožmberk's support for Poděbrady was a serious departure from a long-standing relationship with the Austrian aristocracy and monarchy. He decided that support for his sister did more to enhance the family estates than did traditional political alliances. The Austrian Habsburgs had expected Rožmberk to support their candidate, and now they feared an invasion by Poděbrady linking up with discontented Austrian nobles. To counter the surprise and shock in Austrian and in Catholic circles in general, the Rožmberk officials were put to work to contain the damage. One Rožmberk spokesman, Rupert of Polheim, was called upon to explain. Among other things, he writes, 'the lord [John of Rožmberk] never did want to say "yes" to his election'. Another Rožmberk source, the writer of the *Rožmberk Chronicle*, claimed John had no choice but to vote for Poděbrady, saying:

> This son of a whore [Poděbrady] was elected as King of Bohemia by the city of Prague, by Kostka [of Postupice] and by his other devotees. And the other lords had to agree, having been coerced because he [George] had three executioners standing ready at the town hall.[33]

[31] *Listář a listinář*, 4, p. 435. Compare Skýbová, *Listy*, pp. 16–18.
[32] Rudolf Urbánek, *O volbě Jiřího z Poděbrad za krale českého 2 března 1458* [About the Election of George of Poděbrady as King of Bohemia, 2 March 1458] (Prague: Československý Akademie Věd, 1958), p. 60.
[33] Urbánek, *O volbě*, pp. 65, 87.

Perchta's and John's relationship shows that a nobleman could sacrifice the so-called masculine interests of his dynasty and its political tradition and hopes to his sister's personal happiness. John decided that his father's political distaste for Poděbrady and his family's long-standing bonds to Austria were less important than the need to reorganize his family's finances and, among other things, address his sister's unhappiness. John's alliance with George of Poděbrady was not a temporary event, wrung out of him by force or deception. Rožmberk supported George politically and with his troops until August 1468. His return to the Catholic party and into the camp of Mátyás of Hungary came only after Pope Paul II intervened and the Archbishop of Prague placed an interdict on the Rožmberk estates.[34] By accepting Poděbrady as king and alleviating Perchta's need, John placed sibling feelings before his family's traditional political alignment and honor abroad. His feelings for his sister moved him more than did dynastic politics. John did not react to his sister's assertive actions confronting male prerogatives as though it were a game in which gains for one side, women, entailed a corresponding loss for the other, men. For John the interests of both the women and men of the Rožmberk family were served by subordinating confessional politics and alliances to personal needs.

5. Anéžka, the unmarried sister

Compared to Perchta, Anéžka of Rožmberk lived a life of independence because she chose to remain unmarried. Anéžka left fewer letters than her younger sister, partly because as an unmarried woman she did not have to describe the kind of problems which faced Perchta. The smaller correspondence by and about her reveals a woman of similar energy, autonomy, and self-awareness. An aristocratic woman who neither married nor entered a convent was rare. In his study of the German nobility from the thirteenth to the sixteenth century, Karl-Heinz Spieß found only two cases of single lay noblewomen.[35] From a family's point of view, a single woman represented a dilemma and a risk. She had a right to part of the family inheritance, but if she did not marry in the interests of her family's marriage strategies, her share of the estate potentially fell beyond its control and influence. An independent sister was therefore always a matter of unease for her family. Should she at some time decide to marry and to make her choice of spouse without her

---

[34] Kubíková, *Rožmberské kroniky*, pp. 197–200.
[35] Spieß, *Familie*, pp. 380–81.

family's counsel or consent, her kin had at least lost the opportunity to capitalize on a resource, if not worse. She could marry into a rival family whose political and dynastic interest threatened those of her own family. In the worst case, such a self-reliant marriage meant that the castle or property she inherited passed into the possession of the enemy. Anéžka's success in avoiding marriage reflects her own strong will as well as the sensitivity of her father to her desires.

Anéžka did not see her independence as an act of individualism setting herself apart from her family. In fact she stressed that she had retained the family's estate intact, even while enjoying her share of it. Under Czech custom, when a daughter received her portion of the inheritance she was seen as having withdrawn from the family's economic regime and could make no more claim on its property. Despite having a good and secure stipend of 6,000 groschen a year (the same as Perchta's marriage portion and twice what her father gave himself as retirement income),[36] Anéžka did not take the independent course and disassociate herself from the family jointure (Letter 70). Although her decision to remain unmarried implied a risk to her family, the danger was lessened by her choice to remain within the undivided family property circle.

As an independent woman, Anéžka retained a close relationship to her siblings. Her male kin consented to her ruling over one of its main castles. As she made clear in her last will and testament, Anéžka had been the full heir and administrator of the estate of Třeboň. At the same time she remained an integral member of the Rožmberk family. Her arrangement to have control over her share of the estate but not to be officially separated nor declared economically independent served both her and her family's interests. In a sense she had the best of both worlds. In the end she bequeathed Třeboň to her brother's son, Henry. Her attachment to her family meant that she could call on her father's officials to supply her needs, such as an armed guard or a coach when riding or travelling (Letters 36 and 37). Anéžka's material solidarity with her family reflected her strong emotional feelings towards her kin. Perchta's sorrow troubled Anéžka, as her letters indicate. Her letter of 31 July 1465 shows that Perchta sent her envoys to Anéžka perhaps hoping that they stood a better chance of receiving payment with her sister

---

[36] I assume that the 6,000 groschen she gives away in her testament is the income for the last year of her life. For Ulrich's 3,000 groschen annual income from his estate of retirement, Majdštejn or Dívčí Hrad, see *Listář a listinář*, 4, pp. 425 and 429.

than with her brothers (Letter 45). Even in this case, however, it seems the letter-carrier went home before getting paid.

One requirement of her will, and a significant expense, was her gift of 6,000 groschen to an unnamed charity; the details, which have not survived, she spelled out elsewhere. Anéžka's special plea that her nephew fulfil this bequest suggests he may have found it an unwelcome expenditure. She also felt affection for her servants and stipulated that they all be allowed to stay in her castle for one year after her death so that they could find new living accommodation.

Anéžka's forms of address to her kin reflect close emotional bonds. Although she used the formal 'Your Grace' and 'You' (rather than 'thou') in the text, she addressed her brother John as 'my dear little page', or 'my dear little Johnny', and in a letter to a family official she asked him to 'thank tremendously my dear lord my daddy' (Letters 22, 31, and 49). She was clearly unimpressed by her brother's need to express his aristocratic military prowess: she greeted his statement that he was off on another campaign as the worst possible news and asked him not to go. She then prescribed for him a diet which she hoped would keep him healthy. Her affection extended to her nieces and nephews; as she told her brother John, she especially missed seeing his children (Letters 45 and 49). Anéžka's letters confirm the tight bonding among the children of Ulrich of Rožmberk.

One can understand why August Sedláček, who edited her letters in 1883, called her an Amazonian woman. She pursued her own interests and made her own decisions, and evidently found satisfaction in overseeing the breeding of her cattle, of which she had several kinds. She hunted successfully and conducted her own business with her own seal. She enjoyed the friendship of the men in her family's service (Letter 51), but she also rebuffed her kin and friends when displeased by them. In 1474, Gregory Klaryc, a Rožmberk official, described an incident which admirably shows us Anéžka's spunky independent streak (Letter 66). We are not given the whole picture and there is some confusion in his account. He reported that he arrived at Anéžka's castle Třeboň to carry out his lord's, her nephew's, orders to arrange a banquet for some nobles and maidens, none of whom are identified. When he entered her kitchen she informed him that she had her utensils there and there was no way she was going to remove them or let him remove them. She apparently felt intruded upon and resented having to make her domestic space available so that her nephews could party with their friends.

6. Property and marriage gifts

Access to property played a key role in the lives of both Perchta and Anéžka. Marriage gifts were meant to help defray the costs a bride and her retinue brought to her new household, while also providing for her security should her husband leave her a widow. The property a woman brought into her marriage reflected the status she expected in her new home. Both what she brought and what he added to the marriage, as well as how he handled the property, became extremely important for her livelihood should she become widowed. It was common for the husband's surviving kin to try to get their hands on the widow's property. The competing interests for a woman's share in the family incomes generally caused problems for late medieval European families despite the law's efforts to support women. Complaints about insecure dowries among German aristocratic women were widespread, and in Italy wives found that their security vanished because their husbands dissipated dowry moneys through imprudent and wasteful actions.[37] Probably because of the lengths to which Czech customary law went to protect widows, Perchta's father insisted that the property arrangements of her marriage contract with John of Lichtenštejn were to proceed according to that custom.

Bohemian law described the family patrimony or inheritance as a unit (*rodinný nedíl*) shared by both male and female members, so that a woman saw herself not as a free-loader, but as one who brought her portion of goods, covering her own expenses, and as a person with rights. Inheritance customs resembled the situation in the German states of the Holy Roman Empire of which Bohemia was a member. When Kornel of Všehrd in the late fifteenth century summarized what he had learned about judicial practice, he claimed to be describing old Czech law. According to Všehrd, a daughter had a share, although not one equal to that of her brother, which she could claim as an adult or when her father died. A daughter did share equally any property her family acquired and added to the patrimony during her father's lifetime. If her father had no male

---

[37] For some problems faced by women without property, see Olwen Hufton, *The Prospect before Her: A History of Women in Western Europe. 1500–1800* (New York: HarperCollins, 1996), pp. 67, 70, 73, 90, 125; Spieß, *Familie*, pp. 134–35; Julius Kirshner, 'Wives' Claims against Insolvent Husbands in Late Medieval Italy', in *Women in the Medieval World*, ed. Julius Kirshner and Suzanne Wemple (Oxford: Oxford University Press, 1985), pp. 256–302; and Susan M. Stuard, *A State of Deference: Ragusa/Dubrovnik in the Medieval Centuries* (Philadelphia: University of Pennsylvania Press, 1992), pp. 100–101.

heir, she inherited the whole estate. If she married, a daughter received her share at that time. A father could unilaterally separate his daughter from the patrimony only if he identified her share in a special document. A brother could not on his own separate a sister unless he broke up the family property unit giving each sibling his or her share.

Všehrd stated that if a sister did not receive her portion and separate herself from her brother, he was obliged to provide a suitable place for her to live.[38] The law took special pains to protect a sister from being browbeaten into any action against her interest. She had to appear before the king or the Land court and solemnly swear that she agreed to any property transaction involving her rights, and that she acted freely and with no coercion whatever. The unmarried Anéžka of Rožmberk knew Czech custom and in her last will took pride in the fact that she was free to act while remaining in the family jointure.

Kornel of Všehrd also offers the clearest description of what Czech law called the dowry (*věno*). It was in fact two gifts: one of money which the wife's family gave, and the other the husband's guarantee or lien which he placed on his own property, and which in practice amounted to one and a half times that of the bride's. In Všehrd's words:

> The dowry is a sum of money one-third of the value of what has been designated by the husband or by his kin or by anyone else by means of a bond in the name of the maiden for the benefit of the wife, by registration in the records, or by letter, or by guarantors, or by delivery, and adequately secured on the hereditary property.[39]

In Perchta's marriage contract (Item 2), her family actually designated 60,000 groschen for her as the dowry (*Heratgut*) and her husband, John of Lichtenštejn, added 90,000 as a corollary (*Heimsteuer*) to the gift of her father. The groom then secured the total sum of 150,000 groschen as a mortgage in the name of his wife on a selected property, the castle Steiregg near Linz, Austria. Both father

---

[38] This discussion is based on four late medieval collections of custom described in more detail in Klassen, *Warring Maidens*, pp. 61–77. See also Jan Kapras, 'Manželské právo majetkové dle českého práva zemského' [Marriage Property Law according to the Law of the Czech Land], *Věstník královské české společnosti Nauk. Třida filosoficko-historicko-jazykozpytná*' (Prague, 1908), pp. 7–14. For the Land court's decision, see Josef Emler, ed., *Reliquiae tabularum terrae regni Bohemiae*, 2 vols. (Prague: Clam Martinice, 1870–72), 1, p. 160.

[39] *Všehrd*, p. 216, Kapras, 'Manželské', pp. 31–33.

and husband specified that the money be given to Perchta so that it was seen as her property. In addition to the monetary marriage gift, Perchta could expect one-third of the household goods such as silverware, any cash on hand, grain, and wine. Perchta left all of these household effects behind when she left her husband in 1465 (Letters 39–42 and 61).

Perchta's lack of authority was at the heart of her unhappy marriage. Among the nobility of the Empire, the servants and officials of the husband normally pledged obedience to the new bride. In such cases or in a friendly marriage the question of whether the wife actually received the money into her hands was less important, because the servants and officials followed her orders and wishes, as long as they did not run counter to those of her husband. Perchta lacked a satisfactory procedure for her to access Lichtenštejn funds in order to fulfil her obligations and rights as domestic supervisor of the household. Although her marriage contract promised her an annual income of 15,000 groschen (reduced to 6,000 groschen as long as her family did not deliver the dowry), her access to it was never entirely resolved despite her unflagging efforts. In December 1474 she wrote to her brother-in-law that he was over 37,000 groschen behind in his bi-annual payments (Letter 67).

The means by which her dowry had been secured was also a crucial matter for Perchta. Kornel of Všehrd stressed that the property securing a wife's gift had to be of greater value than the dowry and had to be unencumbered by other obligations to king, church, kin, or creditor. Hence Perchta's father was responsible for seeing to it that the marriage contract looked after these conditions. Unless a will or a marriage agreement stated otherwise, custom gave a husband's surviving kin the right to redeem the property by paying her the full amount of her dowry (both her family's and her husband's contribution). Since the property on which it was secured was to be of greater value, it is understandable that the husband's kin would want to redeem it by paying off the widow and then evict her from the residence. Lichtenštejn's brothers added to Perchta's difficulties by trying to manipulate John and Perchta out of her income and the property which secured it. Perchta's disagreeable relations with her husband's brother meant that her aggravated situation continued even after her family delivered her dowry. Perchta suggested that her brothers-in-law tricked John into mortgaging his property, and teased her with the prospect that her husband's seal was in fact not on the marriage agreement. Several times she asked her kin to check the seals, and when her husband died she asked to have the original contract in her own hands in order to examine it (Letter 58). The contract as preserved was silent on her rights as a widow, but Czech law, which governed her marriage, was not.

Kornel of Všehrd's review of the dowry's immunity was clear; the law did not allow a husband to use his wife's dowry as collateral for his debts. He said that a wife was not a free person, and so the law did not allow her to undertake any liability or encumbrance against her dowry, because the suspicion that she did so under threat from her husband was too real. A court decision in 1495 involving Dorothy of Hostúň and Henry of Strhař illustrated what he meant. Henry had made a loan to Dorothy's husband, who had offered her dowry as surety, and now claimed she owed him money. The judges ruled in Dorothy's favor, saying:

> Dorothy, while in the sustenance of her husband, is the captive of her husband she acted according to her husband's will. For this reason, Dorothy is not liable to Henry for this promise.[40]

The law was determined to give wives surety in case they should become widows. So when Ulrich of Rožmberk stated that the marriage contract for his daughter should follow Bohemian custom, he wanted to give her this kind of protection. Perchta's experience illustrates that no legal safeguards could protect a woman against her husband, or against in-laws who were intent on withholding incomes, where the bailiffs collecting the rents did not answer to her.

7. John of Lichtenštejn

Through Perchta's eyes Lichtenštejn does not appear as an attractive figure. Following her, the nineteenth-century historian František Dvorský portrayed him as unfaithful and dishonorable, as the husband who denied his wife the bliss that comes when a happy couple sits in the presence of their two infant children. The twentieth-century writer, Anna Skýbová, saw Lichtenštejn as more complex. She allowed that Lichtenštejn might have been in substance an evil man, making no effort to overcome his antipathy for Perchta, and that he saw her merely as a source of income and as a means to prop up his material position in his own family without regard for her feelings or welfare. But Skýbová also rightly pointed out that we do not have John's side of the story, because his letters

---

[40] Emler, *Reliquiae*, 1, pp. 138–39, 160.

have not been preserved. She said that Lichtenštejn had his reasons for being alienated from his wife, because her dowry was slow in coming and that 'she dragged his masculine pride all over the kingdom' with her letters.[41]

Perchta married into a family with strong Austrian roots and property there as well as in Moravia. The lords of Lichtenštejn originated in Styria and received their Moravia castle, Mikulov, close to the Austrian border, as a reward for their support for the Czech king, Přemysl Otakar II, in 1249 against the Austrian Habsburgs. With his Austrian connections, John of Lichtenštejn, who shared Mikulov with members of his family but ruled it alone from 1459 to his death in 1474, seemed a logical husband for a daughter of Ulrich of Rožmberk. However, even Ulrich's hopes for political advantages from his daughter's marriage were dashed. Tensions between Rožmberk and his son-in-law escalated rapidly. Sometime after his wedding to Perchta in late 1449, Lichtenštejn shifted political allegiances and supported the Hussite–Polish party headed by George of Poděbrady. Far from finding an ally in Lichtenštejn, Perchta's father found an unpleasant son-in-law and a political enemy. In September 1450 Rožmberk feared military action from the Lichtenštejns was imminent and so he wrote to Ulrich Celský asking for mediation to prevent a clash[42] Lichtenštejn also participated in Poděbrady's military campaign into Austrian lands in 1458 and supported him loyally during his wars with Mátyás Corvinus of Hungary, who with members of the Bohemian nobility attacked Mikulov in 1468, when Perchta no longer lived there. John's political sympathies were not shared by his brothers, Christopher and Henry, who supported the party of Mátyás of Hungary. According to Václav Richter, Lichtenštejn's participation with local bands of robber knights, who terrorized the region, reflected his 'rough and crude' character, which Perchta found hard to tolerate.[43] Richter's conjecture is not substantiated in Perchta's letters, because, whatever else she found intolerable about her husband, she never complained about his warring behavior.

As Lichtenštejn saw it he had done no wrong. From his own perspective things looked quite different from the picture his wife

---

[41] František Dvorský, *Perchta z Rožmberka zvaná bílá paní* [Perchta of Rožmberk, called the White Lady] (Prague, 1874, Matice lidu ročníku VIII. Čislo 2), pp. 79–80, and Skýbová, *Listy*, pp. 26, 35.

[42] *Listář a listinář*, 4, p. 289.

[43] Václav Richter et al., *Mikulov* (Brno: Blok, 1971), pp. 75–82.

painted, even if we use Perchta as our source for his case (Letter 15). He likely found Perchta's correspondence irritating but it is doubtful if he felt his self-esteem wounded by it. He had entered into a property arrangement with the Rožmberk family by marrying a Rožmberk woman. He had a wife and he anticipated having a limited use of her dowry. He had done what was expected of him once he had honorably slept with Perchta that one night in October 1449. No one claimed he had not fulfilled the contract's provisions. The Rožmberks had delayed five years before fulfilling what the contract required of them. It is true that he could have dealt with her most pressing complaints and his peers expected him to provide her with an income despite her family's dereliction. However, that meant using his own family's funds and because he shared the family property in jointure with other members of his family he was not free to allocate resources as he might have wished.

He had brought Perchta to his castle, but she was not content to simply live there; she expected domestic authority and insisted on getting his attention. He had no interest in her and she probably bored him with her repeated requests for companionship. Mostly when two persons share a sexual passion for each other they seek each other's company. This desire and passion was lacking in Lichtenštejn. He sired two children but, according to Perchta, beyond that he refused to spend time with her. One of Perchta's attendants, Šiermarka, informed Henry of Rožmberk that Lichtenštejn struck Perchta physically (Letter 18), which in the fifteenth century was excused by ecclesiastical and secular authorities. Most important, he had not committed himself to being a friend or a lover to his wife and it had not been an expressed condition of the marriage. His wedding was a step he took in response to counsel and prodding from kin and friends to help out the Lichtenštejn family estate. That a number of his aristocratic peers intervened with him to improve his treatment of Perchta shows, however, that his neglect of his bride exceeded even male tolerance for how one mistreated one's wife, at least if she were a Rožmberk daughter.

In sum, the Rožmberk sisters' identity was firmly rooted in their family of birth, and, while they acted with considerable self-reliance, both sisters maintained strong family connections through writing letters to their father and brothers. The family was especially important to Perchta when she found herself in the hostile environment of her own marriage. Her memories of her childhood upbringing and her relations with her father and siblings provided her with the resources for surviving. In her family she developed attitudes of responsibility and independence. Her sister Anéžka, who remained unmarried, retained her bond with her ancestral home with less effort. Czech property custom allowed her to separate her share of the patrimony and live on her own with a generous income, and although she had her own castle as a residence, she was emphatic about her desire to remain part of the Rožmberk kindred and economy. Both were intelligent, capable, and energetic women, but their sense of self grew out of their experience of growing up in a family which continued to nurture them as adults.

The Correspondence of
Perchta and Anéžka of Rožmberk *ca.* 1448–1488

1. *Anéžka and Perchta of Rožmberk write to their brother Henry of Rožmberk that they look forward to his return and describe their contact with animals in the yard of their castle.*

Early February, sometime in the 1440s, Český Krumlov[1]
Czech   *AČ*, no. 3

Let this letter be given to the noble lord Lord Henry of Rožmberk, our dear brother.

We send you our prayers, noble lord, dear brother, and we thank Your Grace very much for the greetings in the packet, and especially for the welcome word that you are returning to us this Shrovetide. Yet everyone looks on the gloomy side[2] [saying] that you will not come. Despite this, we continue to believe that you will not betray us, because if you don't come, those greetings in the packet do not mean anything. And sister says that the big ox always milks the cows in the sick room, expecting you with milk.[3] And we continue to ask you, for God's sake, that you return to us at Carnival. Given in Krumlov the Monday after the feast of St. Dorothy [6 February] under the steps leading to the creamery.

Anéžka and Perchta of Rožmberk.

2. *Betrothal agreement between Ulrich of Rožmberk and John of Lichtenštejn for John to marry Perchta of Rožmberk. It followed Czech custom in which the husband gave one and a half times the amount of the bride's dowry. The marriage was considered sealed once the couple had shared a bed on the first night.*

9 February 1449, Český Krumlov
German   *Listář a listinář*, 4, 9–11

We, Ulrich of Rožmberk, acknowledge and make public with this letter that we have made an agreement with the noble lord, Lord John of Lichtenštejn of Mikulov,[4] and have betrothed our daughter,

---

[1] The letters simply employ 'Krumlov' for the town that in 1259 was identified as Český Crumlov. See *Historischen Stätten Böhmen und Mähren,* ed. Joachim Bahlcke, Winfried Eberhard, and Miloslav Polívka (Stuttgart: Alfred Kroner, 1998), p. 53.

[2] Lit. wishes us evil.

[3] The original Czech is obscure, *žet' vždycky ten vůl velké v špitàle dojí čekajic tebe s mlekem.*' Most likely this refers to a growing calf that is resisting being weaned and takes its milk from cows or wants someone to give it milk from a container.

[4] The main Lichtenštejn castle in Moravia near the border with Austria.

the virgin Perchta, promising to give her as an honorable spouse to him, according to the law of the land of Bohemia. We shall give and want to give as lawful dowry for our daughter, the virgin Perchta, 60,000 good large groschen of Czech Prague coins or the equivalent in Hungarian or Rhine gulden or in good small pennies equal to the value of the aforesaid groschen at that time in the land of Bohemia or Austria. We shall provide and want to provide him and his heirs with a promissory bond for the aforesaid 60,000 groschen, according to the same terms of the note under his seal which the aforesaid Lord John sent us. We shall deliver and want to deliver the same promissory bond fully prepared and sealed according to the above-mentioned lord, Lord John of Lichtenštejn and his heirs, within the next eight weeks, right after the above-named Lord John and our above-named daughter have honorably slept together.[5]

Lord John, in turn, has committed himself and promised to give our aforementioned virgin daughter 90,000 good Czech groschen[6] or its equivalent as the lawful counterpart of her dowry. The above lord, Lord John of Lichtenštejn, shall offer and give to the above named virgin, Perchta, his castle Steiregg[7] from his property and revenues, providing her with an annual income of 15,000 groschen a year for the 60,000 groschen dowry and the 90,000 counterpart, as the letter of marriage which was drawn up according to the note that we have written him under our seal and which he shall provide us when needed clearly stipulates. Similarly, the above-named Lord John shall prepare the marriage letter together with the title deed in the same eight weeks after the said Lord John has honorably slept with our above-named daughter. Then, each party shall deliver without guile all the above letters together with the agreement, within eight weeks, to the other party in the Krumlov castle.

We or our heirs shall honorably and conscientiously deliver the above virgin Perchta, our daughter, to the above Lord John of Lichtenštejn, on the first Sunday before St. Gall's day [16 October] in our castle Krumlov or within eight miles thereabouts. Should it happen that we, the above-named Ulrich of Rožmberk, or our heirs, do not deliver or give our above-named virgin daughter Perchta to

---

[5] The original German is *'eelichen beieinander gelegen sein'*.

[6] On 12 October 1449 Ulrich and Henry of Rožmberk pledged to deliver to the Steiregg castle 3000 groschen twice a year if they had not delivered the full amount of the dowry within one year. *Listář a listinář*, 4, p. 109.

[7] One of the main Lichtenštejn castles near Linz, Austria.

the lord, Lord John of Lichtenštejn, within this time period as spec-ified above, or should the marriage dissolve and fail to take place as described above, then we and our heirs will default the above 60,000 groschen to the aforesaid Lord John of Lichtenštejn and his heirs, which we shall pay and want conscientiously to pay and reimburse to the above Lord John of Lichtenštejn and his heirs within the following two months without fail, including their expenses. Should there be a lawsuit claiming that we, Ulrich of Rožmberk, have not carried out these things, and allowed them to lapse and have not done what is written above, so that You or Your heirs suffer damages, as may happen, all these damages we shall provide and want to provide and to return them, together with the main gift of 60,000 groschen. They shall claim it from us and from all our heirs, whoever they may be, and from all our property and possessions, without exception, whatever it is called, and wherever it may be, and whether we are alive or dead. Or should it happen that we fail to prepare, without explanation, the dowry promissory note for Lord John of Lichtenštejn (if he is not alive, for his heirs) within the above-mentioned eight weeks after our daughter and Lord John have honorably slept together according to the require-ments of the note which the above-named Lord John wrote and sent us under his seal, and he or his heirs suffer damages, as it happens, these damages we, by our faith, pledge to reimburse faithfully and conscientiously; he shall have this with us and in the same way with our heirs and upon all our property and possessions, wherever it is, without exception, whether we are alive or dead. Should it happen that the above-named lord, Lord John of Lichtenštejn, or the above-named virgin our daughter, Perchta, should die, God forbid, before they have honorably slept together, then all above terms and writing about the above marriage are null and void and have no power or effect and neither party is obligated to the other, without fault. This we, the above Ulrich of Rožmberk, issue as notice together with this note of understanding, sealed with this our pressed seal, and the noble lord, Lord John of Lichtenštejn, has also had his seal pressed to this letter of understanding. This took place in Krumlov on Sunday after Candlemas of our beloved Lady, in 1449.

3.   *Perchta of Rožmberk writes her brother Henry what seems to be either nonsense, a humorous note, or an allegorical message in which the carnival fool represents her husband. Her letter is apparently an answer to his letter which has not been preserved.*

Friday, 1449, Mikulov[8]
German   *AČ* no. 9

To the noble lord, Lord Henry of Rožmberk, my dear brother. Willingly in your service, dear brother. I am sending you my carnival fool; he has eaten much sweetness[9] for me in his fool's wisdom, and I [want to] let you know that he slanders you in front of my servants and other good people; [he says that] you have made him an empty promise. I should not portray him to you as a bad person when I answer you in this letter and ask you to punish him and not to let him out of your hands, but to tie his hands behind his back and lead him to Krumlov and place him in the honey pot from which he licks; then I will send for him again. I trust you, dear brother, to do this when he is of maximum use. I do not want to put into writing what he has said about you, and if you punish him for it, I will tell you more about him, should you, God willing, come to me. If you place him into the honey pot, do not drown him in it; if he is able [let him] serve another year as the carnival fool. For this reason Šiermarka[10] asks you to spare him because of his age and his bald head, which at the same time indicate wisdom. Nourish him with it as Šiermarka has nourished him. He knows well what this was, and has had his pleasure with it.[11] Give him a well-fried mouse so that he does not spit out his teeth. Please, dear brother, give him the letter so that he can read it through himself. Given in Mikulov.

Perchta of Rožmberk, wife of Lord John of Lichtenštejn.

---

[8]   Her husband's main castle and residence in Moravia near the border with Austria.

[9]   References to sweetness and honey may refer to court gossip to which the 'fool' is privy.

[10]   Lit. *die Schirmerin*, or the Schirmer woman, in Czech, *Šiermarka*. The Schirmer family were friends of the Rožmberks. See *Listář a listinář Oldřicha z Rožmberka 1418–1462* [Letters and Documents of Ulrich of Rožmberk 1418–1462] vol. 3, ed. Blažena Rynešova (Prague: Státní Tiskárna, 1929), p. 25.

[11]   It is not clear to what she is referring. The reference to the 'well-fried mouse' may be a request that her brother treat the fool kindly.

4. *Šiermarka and Machna Koník, two ladies in Perchta's retinue who have accompanied her from Český Krumlov. They express their close feelings for her brother, John of Rožmberk. Machna has been gone from the Rožmberks, for about two months and poignantly laments her separation from her son.*

November–December 1449, Mikulov
Czech   *AČ* no. 10

We offer our incessant, obedient prayers. We would like to hear that all is going well with Your Grace. Thanks be to God, all is well with us and, dear lord, we very much long to see Your Grace. I greatly regret that I cannot speak with Your Grace alone; it seems to me like a hundred years since I last saw Your Grace, and like a thousand years since I saw my son. And although I do not see you, I nevertheless do not forget you. And please do not forget me and the expenses I have [incurred] even though I have served only a short time.[12] I let Your Grace know that for me [things] have slightly improved here with the lady, and that we play dice but that we have not learned anything better from the Germans. And [my] dear lord, let a prayer be said from me for my son, and I pray that you will be loving towards my son, so that I will not go out of my mind here. I only hold onto [the prospect of] seeing Your Grace. I have already spoken enough madness. I, Machna Koník, offer my prayer, my dear lord. Given in Mikulov on Sunday.
The maiden Šiermarka and the maiden[13] Machna.

5. *Perchta of Rožmberk, in her first letter to her father Ulrich of Rožmberk after her wedding, expresses her longing for him.*

November–December 1449, Mikulov
Czech   *AČ*, no. 11

Let [this letter] be given to my father, the noble lord, Lord Ulrich of Rožmberk. I send my prayers, noble lord! And I would be truly happy to hear that all is going well with you; I also thank the Lord

---

[12] Because she is in Rožmberk service, her expenses must be covered by him. The references to the Germans is to the people of the Lichtenštejn court where the language was German.

[13] Without supporting evidence, František Dvorský, *Perchta z Rožmberka zvaná bílá paní* [Perchta of Rožmberk, called the White Lady] (Prague, 1874, Matice lidu ročníku VIII. islo 2), p. 24, claims the writer was a widow, although the term *panna* was used to designate an unmarried woman or virgin.

God [that] I am well, except that I cannot stop longing for Your Grace, and most heartily I ask to see Your Grace, for I would like very much to see for myself how Your Grace is doing. And dear lord, I beseech Your Grace not to forget me, but to please be loving towards me, for I would never want to lose Your Grace; I would always want to do everything that is pleasing to Your Grace. And with this I commend Your Grace to the Loving God. Given in Mikulov.

Perchta of Rožmberk.

6.   *Perchta of Rožmberk to her father Ulrich, indicating that she has made an effort to see him in Vienna and hinting at her troubled relationship with her husband.*

11 January 1450, Mikulov
Czech   *AČ* no. 12

Let this be given to the noble lord, Lord Ulrich of Rožmberk, my lord and my dear father.

Noble and dear lord, I send my prayers. In true faith, I was glad to hear that Your Grace returned in good health from his Royal Grace,[14] and also that, as Your Grace has written me, Your Grace insisted that I come to see you in Vienna; I dedicated myself to this very end and looked forward to it exceedingly, especially because I only too gladly wanted to see Your Grace as I need to see you. But then it was impossible; still, I very much thank Your Grace for the messenger whom Your Grace sent to me. Your Grace writes to me that Your Grace hopes to visit his Royal Grace as soon as possible, and that Your Grace would like to see me there. But, I am afraid that Your Grace only wants to see me [in company] with him [her husband]. And I ask that you will please forgive me, for writing to Your Grace that I did not believe Your Grace, for I would like very much to see Your Grace. The old lady[15] sends a big prayer to Your Grace. And with it I commend Your dear Grace to the Lord God. Given in Mikulov on Sunday after the [feast of] three kings [6 January].

Perchta of Rožmberk.

---

[14]   King Frederick in Vienna, who at this time was the guardian of Ladislav. Ulrich was the most powerful baron leading the pro-Habsburg forces which were in the midst of negotiating with the Hussite party.

[15]   Possibly her mother-in-law.

7. *Perchta of Rožmberk reveals to her father Ulrich that she is unhappy in her marriage because she does not have the authority nor the income that she expected as a wife, and that her husband's family is quarreling. She points out that she has told only her father and her brother about her complaint.*

20 February 1450, no place
Czech   *AČ* no. 13

Let this be given to my dear lord, my father, Lord Ulrich of Rožmberk.

And dear lord! That which I wrote you in my first letter, that I am doing well, is unfortunately not so; would that I was doing well. On the contrary, I am doing very badly. And the complaint I bring before Your Grace is that I am in such a disorderly residence that there is no way I can get used to it. I am a veritable beggar of that lady and have to wait for everything from her hands. Still, I would gladly go on waiting, if only the things I need were given, although in the past I have received what I needed. Because it is an unbelievable matter that that woman should [be allowed to] manage those things which she has under her control and in her hands. I could perhaps suffer all this easier, except, dear lord, it is very difficult for me because they [her in-laws] are very bad towards one another, since unfortunately now the lord [John] has acted against his uncle, and I am afraid that he will not be able to put it right without shame to himself; they are to settle the matter at the court in Vienna, and each party is to have its kinsmen and friends [witness] against each other, and I anticipate he will request your Grace's counsel on this. You should know that he rode to Vienna on Shrove Sunday and that no one, not even Šek,[16] could hold him back. He went alone without his good people; what he wants to do, no one knows. Therefore, dear lord, you should know that I am in great sorrow and in great need; therefore dear lord, I ask Your Grace, if it is possible, to make some arrangement so that I could soon meet with you. And as I previously wrote to Your Grace, asking that he [her husband] admit me into his presence, on the basis of my humble request, so it seems to me, if Your Grace will request it, that he will not refuse Your Grace in this matter, [even] if it seems to be unlikely to Your Grace; but I ask Your Grace to send Rús[17] to me, so that he can look over my living quarters. I would have written to Your Grace

---

[16] An important official, possibly the governor in Lichtenštejn's castle, Mikulov. Dvorský, *Perchta*, p. 27.

[17] John Rús of Čemin, a Rožmberk official.

a long time ago, but I continually expected improvement, and did not want to trouble Your Grace with it; but now Šek has advised me against keeping silence and has advised me to request Your Grace to send Rús to me. I ask Your Grace to comfort me in this, in my great sorrow, and send him to me, that he may see with his eyes how they treat me, for at present I need this greatly; I would like to know Your Grace's will about how I am supposed to exist in this [situation]; but you should know already that I feel exceedingly lonely and desperate. And dear lord, I trust that Your Grace will subject me only so much to their will. I wrote, trusting Your Grace, that you would like to improve my disorderly living conditions so that I should not be in such great sorrow. I wrote to all that I am doing well, except to Your Grace and to lord Henry; and I wrote this, or my Henry [secretary] wrote this for me (but this will not be made known). And I ask that you please read it yourself and do not show it to anyone.

8.   *Ulrich of Rožmberk writes to Perchta about political events in the land and his reluctance to intervene in the lordship of John of Lichtenštejn, her husband. He asks his daughter to refrain from making public her discontent.*

26 February 1450, Český Krumlov
Czech   *AČ* no. 14

Lady Perchta, dear daughter! When you wrote me in Vienna and here, you asked to meet with me and your brothers, and if that should not be possible, that I should send Rús to you. I understood it all well and am letting it be known that this Saturday I leave from here for Zvíkov, where I am supposed to meet with Lord Aleš[18] and with other mediators. From there, I will go to Plzeň for the Diet,[19] so that we will not be able to meet at this time. Also it does not seem proper that I should send Rús to you now; but, God willing, when I return again, I want to think it over and send for you, so that you can come to me and so that I can speak with you myself about this matter, and, God willing, you will be able to talk with your brothers.[20] Therefore

---

[18] Aleš of Šternberk, a leading baron of the Hussite–Polish party opposed to Rožmberk's Catholic–Austrian party, but with whom Ulrich was in frequent communication on both public and domestic matters.

[19] This was a major assembly of Rožmberk's party, including Frederick the duke of Saxony, in an alliance directed against George of Poděbrady. *Listář a listinář*, 4, pp. 171–73.

[20] The Czech *bratrany*, or the sons of one's brother, but the context indicates that he meant her brothers.

dear daughter, do not at this time speak with anyone about this matter, and when, God willing, we meet, we will take counsel and I will take action on this matter, so that, God willing, this affair will come to a happy conclusion. I ask you please to pray to the loving Lord God for us, that he will deign to help us so that the disorders in the land will be stopped, and that he will give us that which will be for our soul's salvation. Given in Krumlov, Friday 26 February 1450.

9. *Perchta of Rožmberk writes to her father Ulrich about her concern for him and asks him to intervene with her husband. She repeats that her poverty is caused by her mother-in-law. She asks that Ulrich pay her messenger.*

16 May 1450, Mikulov
Czech *AČ* **no. 15**

May this be given to the noble lord, Lord Ulrich of Rožmberk, my dear father.

I send you my prayers, my dear noble lord! And dear lord, I would most gladly hear that Your Grace is well. And they certainly told me evil tales about Your Grace; that Your Grace had died. I was greatly grieved by this, for I care greatly about Your Grace's welfare and I ask Your Grace always to tell anyone whom You might meet, who might see me, how Your Grace is doing. The meeting with Your Grace, which I requested earlier, will perhaps not be possible, because I heard here that there may be a battle. But I pray Your Grace, dear lord, for God's sake, do not forget me, and please send someone to me, someone whom I might entrust with information about how I am doing, and secondly, who might see with his [own] eyes; for I suffer great destitution because of this sinful mother [-in-law] so much that I feel very lonely and desperate in this [situation]. And I ask Your Grace, please arrange matters with him [husband] so that things might go differently for me than they are at present. I ask Your Grace, please forgive me for writing to you so often, for I do not know of anyone with whom I might better take refuge than with Your Grace. I ask Your Grace, please do not forget me. I always favor Your Grace, and would like to continue to do so. I ask Your Grace, please order that recompense be given to the messenger for the journey. With this I commend Your Grace to God.

Given in Mikulov on Saturday after the Lord's Ascension.
Perchta of Rožmberk.

10.   *Perchta of Rožmberk to her brother Henry asking him for compassion in her distress and poverty. She acknowledges that he finds her news annoying, but stresses that others too are reporting what they have seen of her living conditions.*

3 July 1450, Mikulov
Czech   *AČ* no. 16

I send my prayers to the noble lord, Lord Henry of Rožmberk, the noble lord and my dear brother. I was glad to hear that Your Grace returned home in good health. As Your Grace requested me to write, indicating that You would be glad to act once you return from Pelhřimov, to arrange for me to meet with Your Grace: dear Lord Henry, have compassion on me for the dear God's sake and please take action as soon as possible, and help me [to gain relief] for a while from this family for God's sake; otherwise [I shall die] and nothing will be left to you except to pay for my soul's salvation[21] as one does in order to free a sinful soul from hell. Also, you write to me that I should now stop all writing and messages, and that you know why you forbid me. Dear lord, I will gladly do it. Does not the report which Lord Aleš [of Šternberk] made for me please the lord? Dear lord, please know that the idea that I might have asked him to take it to the lord, did not start with me, because he said many things to me, about what my conditions were, which he had learned from others, not from me; also, he was with us for a good while, and I could not deny all that he saw with his own eyes. And when I could not deny it, only then did I agree that he could let the lord [Rožmberk] know, for he said to me: 'Do you agree or do you not agree that he desires and intends to take this to the lord?' In doing this, he does a service for the lord, for no one at all can believe it, except he who sees me in this [condition]. Now they have left me in distress, he and his mother having departed and left me with the servants, and for myself, I do not know what to do with those whom I still have at home. They govern me more than I govern them. I have a complaint, dear brother; he bade his mother give something to me when he was going away, and she did go away but gave me

---

[21]   The Czech, *zádušie*, refers to material gifts made to the Church or to the poor on behalf of the deceased. Both priests and lay people could be asked to pray for the benefit of a dead person's soul. See John Klassen, 'Gifts for the Soul and Social Charity in Late Medieval Bohemia', *Materielle Kultur und Religiöse Stiftung im Spätmittelalter. Veröffentlichungen des Instituts für Mittelalterliche Realkunde Österreichs* 12 (Vienna, 1990), pp. 63–81.

nothing. And I believe to God that I am acting just as you asked me to; therefore, I believe Your Grace, that you will hear my complaint[22] for the sake of good people. Dear Brother! I am now sending you a shirt. I ask that you will please wear it for my sake, although I am an old woman. Dear lord! Since I am always asking you to allow me to come sooner, let someone be sent to me soon. Also you ask me to pray to God on your behalf; I could never forget you, not even in my imperfect prayers. Also, you, only Your Grace, and no one else, have a letter from me sent via Lord Aleš. With this I commend Your Grace to God. Given in Mikulov on Friday before St. Procop's day [4 July].

Perchta of Rožmberk.

11. *Perchta of Rožmberk, writing to her brother Henry, confirms that he has taken action on her behalf and that a high Austrian official is also involved. She fears her brother's censure for writing and indicates that her life is in danger. She wants to go to her dowry castle.*

12 November 1450 Vienna
Czech   *AČ* **no. 19**

Let this be given to the noble lord, Lord Henry, my dear brother.

I send you my prayers, noble lord and my dear brother! I will be glad to hear that you are all doing well. My dear lord, I am informing you of these things, about which you spoke to my lord [husband]; please understand that things are going very badly for me; since then I have borne much grief, and heard some evil words from him. I do not understand why, since he was the one who took the initiative. But please understand that Lord Ebrštorf[23] is proceeding with great diligence in this matter; I suspect that if nothing [comes] of his efforts, then things will remain the same. Therefore dear lord! I ask that Your Grace please write urgently to Lord Ebrštorf so that he might push hard in this [matter] and in everything that I need; for if he does not [succeed] in this, you must know that unfortunately it will not go well [here]. And so I hope, [but] from what I can understand regrettably I will have a miserable time with him. Therefore I believe, dear lord, that you will not blame me when I write Your Grace about all this, for I do it out of

---

[22] Lit. give me the use of this.

[23] Sigismund of Eberdorf was a high official in the service of Emperor Frederick III of Austria. *Listář a listinář*, 4, p. 73.

great faith. Also, I utterly cannot understand why he might want to dismiss me to Steiregg.[24] If he does, I will then go to my mother.[25] When it is more convenient for me, I will send a messenger to you immediately. Šiermarka also sends you her many prayers. Given in Vienna.

Perchta of Rožmberk.

Postscript

Dear lord, I ask you, please take some action, so that I may go to Steiregg at the first opportunity. Do what you can as soon as possible, for unfortunately I have learned something which it is definitely not good for one to make public or to write about; there can be nothing worse than this. And I would give a great deal to be able to let you know about this. You should know, unfortunately, that it may concern my life. So for God's sake do not delay in this. And if dear God allows me to meet with you, if I survive to see this through in good health, I will let you know what is happening and you will be amazed.

12. *Ulrich of Rožmberk writes to Perchta urging her to be happy. He indicates that he has provided her with spending money while her dowry remains unpaid.*

14 November 1450, Český Krumlov

Czech   *AČ* **no. 21**

Noble lady, Lady Perchta of Lichtenštejn and of Mikulov, my dear daughter.

Dear Daughter, I am letting you know that, thank God, we all, with your brothers and sisters, are well, which is something I would like to wish for you also. Therefore dear daughter, keep yourself well and put off all sorrows; be happy and in good spirits; I believe that you will. And I hope that, God willing, we will soon see each other. I send you ten Hungarian gulden for your needs. May God allow you to tell us you are doing better. And I ask you to let me know how you are, for I would very gladly see that you are well.

Postscript

Also Henry, your brother, told me you have spent almost all the money which you were given here. I did not know this. Given the Saturday after St. Martin's day [11 November].

---

[24] The castle near Linz, Austria, on which John of Lichtenštejn had secured her dowry.

[25] Perchta most likely meant her husband's mother since her own was no longer living.

13.   *Perchta of Rožmberk to her father Ulrich, describing intimate details of her life including her loneliness, the danger to her life, her desire for her husband's companionship and her shame because of his public disdain for her. She appeals to her father on the basis of her rights as his child.*

22 November 1450, no place
Czech   *AČ* no. 20

To the noble lord, Lord Ulrich of Rožmberk, my dear lord father.

I send you my service, Your Grace, noble lord, and I would like to know that everything is well with you. Dear lord! I want to let you know that I am a lonely and woeful woman, too much deserted by you and by all, and I believe before God that I have done nothing to Your Grace to deserve it. It would be better that the day that saw me born had rather seen me dead, and Your Grace would have greater happiness from that than you can expect from me if you do not provide for me. Therefore, dear lord, dear father, have compassion on me, as a father towards his children, and bear in mind, dear lord, that it was not my wish to be married. And I have called for and pleaded for help, which is my right as a child of its father; and remember, dear lord, your own blood-kin, for the sake of God's mercy. Deserted, I have written [my] brother and have often sent messages, requesting that he take them to Your Grace; I do not know if he has done this, for my messages have brought me no assistance, not even after what your servants have seen with their own eyes. Therefore, dear lord, I want to describe somewhat more urgently what is important to me so that Your Grace might know that I am not exaggerating,[26] and so that I will not be vainly asking you for immediate help. And dear lord, please know for certain that I have often been warned by good and honorable people that I should be on guard against his mother as well as against him. The word is that they intend to poison me, and that this would have happened to me a long time ago, but they dare not do this to me because of my servants, fearing that they would inform Your Grace about it. And if he had dared to accomplish this, [but] for Your Grace, he would gladly have sent everyone away, so that he might be able to achieve it alone. I myself understand well that they would gladly bid me farewell from this world; people speak about this publicly. I have let [my] brother know about this, asking that he

---

[26] Lit. acting in vain.

listen to it, and that you do not entrust my life to him. If it were known that you understand the situation, even he would not dare do anything to me. Moreover, please understand that he shows me great hatred, that if he sees me anywhere he flees from me, and this I can readily write as the complete truth, that since Christmas he has spoken with me only once, and when he did it was only because of Špán.[27] He never comes to sleep with me. And I have tried everything; I followed him into the cellar, into the kitchen, and I even walked into the horse stable, the only place I was able to track him down, to get him to speak with me, but he fled from me while many people, both good and bad, saw it. For me this is so sad and such a shame that it is a wonder my heart is not broken.

Perchta of Rožmberk.

14. *Perchta of Rožmberk to her brother Henry, expressing her belief in the Virgin Mary, while expecting concrete help from Henry. She challenges him to protect her. She indicates that she is drafting a last will and asks that her letter be kept secret.*

November–December 1450, Mikulov
Czech   *AČ* **no. 23**

Noble lord, Lord Henry of Rožmberk, my dear brother.

I send you my prayers, my dear noble lord and brother. And I know well how to write my prayer and I pray for you now in the name of God and of the mother of God, that he might take pity on me and take action so that I might meet with you as soon as possible, and that he [her husband] might do this for the salvation of my and for his [own] soul and for the sake of my life. For it seems to me that on this earth I could have no better or more honorable helper for this than you: I saw something, about which it is not proper to write, especially if I may not see you again, and I am sick from the shock and from grief. Therefore, dear brother, I beseech you not to desert me and let me meet with you again; for already something very evil has happened, [and I] fear something even worse, dear brother, should this [business] lead to my death. And I entrust and commit my soul to you, a dear brother, that you will not forget it; otherwise my soul will be very forsaken. And if I gave instructions for my soul to my maidens and servants who work faithfully with me in the midst of my powerlessness, I commend them along with myself in

---

[27] Špán of Barštejn and of Záhoří was an official with the Rožmberks. Dvorský, *Perchta*, p. 79.

this [situation]. However, I am not heavy-hearted now, except for the great shock I experienced, but I am making my last will in case it should happen that I never see you again. None of my retinue knows about what is troubling me, except Šiermarka only; so should you see it as a good thing to tell the lord [father], tell him; if not, then act as it seems best to you. [Given] in Mikulov.

Perchta of Rožmberk.

Postscript

But I do not intend to tell this to father or to anyone before I tell it to you; and I ask you not to expect[28] any more about this until God gives me health; for whatever I have sent, some good person has lent me [the money]. Also, the messenger is not to tell anyone that he came from me, but to say that he was sent from lord Puchoměř.[29] I ask you, please, let no one answer this letter, except for you yourself with your own hand, and let me know the day on which you might arrive.

15.   *Perchta of Rožmberk writes to her brother Henry about threats to her life and her fear of losing her own servants. She describes her husband's indifference and lack of care during the birth of their child, and the help she received from servants. She relates her husband's own unhappiness in the marriage. She expresses concern over the dowry contract and wonders if she is again pregnant.*

December 1450, Mikulov
Czech   *A Č* no. 24

Noble lord, Lord Henry of Rožmberk, my dear brother, I send you my prayers, noble lord and dear brother. I was glad to hear that you were doing well, but I am not doing well, for unfortunately my living conditions have not improved; in truth, I came [back] here just as I did earlier and I fear that it may perhaps be worse. I fear that I may lose my life suddenly, although I would be happy to fulfill your command; and you commanded me not to die. Dear brother, I am very thankful that you wrote to my lord because of my maidens, for I missed them so much. You pleased me very much with this message; I cannot express my gratitude to you enough. I was beginning to despair in case you did not write to him.

---

[28]   Lit. let me send you.
[29]   George of Puchheim was the butler in the imperial Austrian court. *Listář a listinář*, vol. 4, p. 345.

And as my lord [husband] writes to Your Grace about my maidens, that he did not intend to act against your will: please do not believe him, for he had every intention of sending them away. When his brother came to Mikulov to call for me, he [his brother] talked about them with someone, [saying] that my husband wanted to send them away without delay. And when I learned of this, I immediately wrote to Lord Eberštorf,[30] who replied to me that my husband fully intended to do it, but he had not done so only because he [Eberštorf] had strongly advised him not to do so unless he first let you know. Dear brother! It seems to me that if that had happened, I would have been deeply sad at heart, for I still have no greater pleasure than these maidens give me.

I have heard that they are preparing two chambermaids[31] for me. Everybody who wishes me well advises me that, if it should come to that, it would not be in my own interest to take them. Dear brother! He [her husband] writes regarding my delivery that if you could make an agreement with your uncle,[32] he [her husband] would like to take proper care of my affairs. I have little hope in him [husband], for if he once showed little concern for me, he now shows even less. And he had agreed with you that he would arrange for them [the maidens] to be with me during the birth and lying in, [but] he did not do so, and I got only what Eberštorf took upon himself to arrange. And he did not want to give me a wagon to carry the things which I had brought with me myself, and he sent me away from Vienna so that I had nothing to eat, and had it not been for Kodaur,[33] I do not know how I would have arrived [at home].

And dear brother! As I wrote earlier that something had happened to me, now I will tell you something. When someone spoke to my wicked lord, and suggested to him that he should live with me differently, if not for my sake, nor for that of my kin, then [at least] for the sake of other people, because people are talking a lot about how terrible things are for me, he replied that nothing in the world can make him relate to me happily, and, cursing all those who had

---

[30] An official in the service of Emperor Frederick III of Austria.

[31] The Czech, *kaczes*, literally means ducks, but is also the abbreviation for 'Katherine', a nickname for female servants which seems to fit the context here.

[32] Because Perchta's dowry has not been delivered, her husband wants her kinsman, George of Kravař, to provide Perchta with the physical needs in childbirth. George several times came to her aid. See Letters 30 and 32 below. Since Perchta mixes her tenses, it is not clear whether she is referring to her husband's intentions in a future pregnancy, or his unfulfilled promises in the one just past.

[33] A Rožmberk servant.

counseled him to get married, that he never had such an intention, but they compelled him to it; that if he should not see me for a year, he would not remember me at all, and that when he sees me, he greatly fears me. This man questioned him as to why he spoke this way, or if he finds any fault with me; and he told him that he finds absolutely no fault with me and that...[34] he does not blame me, except that he cannot happily live with me; that as long as he has lived he has not been loving to any woman. It is not proper to write about the rest; he talked about himself indecently and desperately. I could not believe that he would say this about himself. But I certainly experienced it, my dear brother; therefore I am writing to you, for I trust you above all others and ask your advice in this. What shall I do about this? I was greatly saddened by the conversation; because I am utterly weighed down by how badly things are going for me. And so, dear brother, I bid farewell. Deal with this as seems fitting. With this I commend you to dear God. [Given] in Mikulov.

Perchta of Rožmberk.

Postscript

Dear brother! Examine carefully the document in which my dowry was drawn up, because they say to me here that the document which was made is not valid, that if the Lord God should not preserve my lord [husband], William, his brother, would be able to litigate everything away from me. Also examine the seal, for the lord has Lord William's seal, and see if he did not attach William's seal instead of his own. And dear lord, you should know that my lord is preparing to spend the whole year in Vienna and lord Henry has assumed authority over the estate; so I fear that I will be even less happy.

I want to tell you about my womb. At this time I do not know anything for certain, except that just like the first time, I fear there is nothing there and I am not pregnant. My dear brother! I trust that you will not forget me, for I have placed my hope first in the loving God and then in you; therefore, I trust that you will not forget me. And I also do not forget you in my imperfect prayers, and especially now, when I care so much for you. Remember that a mass is served for you every Saturday. If you cannot go to mass at least always sing seven Hail Marys. You must know that I want to send my messenger to you as soon as possible.

---

[34] At this point the manuscript is unreadable because of a fold and extensive wear.

16.   *Perchta of Rožmberk writes to her father Ulrich about the dismissal of a servant loyal to her and of the uproar it caused. She claims her poverty is now well known in Moravia and Austria. She repeats earlier pleas for help, asks him to employ the dismissed servant, and brings her cause before God. She describes a conversation between her servant and a servant of her father's.*

31 December 1450, Valtice[35]
Czech   *AČ* no. 25

I send you my prayers, dear noble lord. My heart would be happy to learn that Your Grace is well and healthy. O dear lord! But I live like such a poor wretch; it is a wonder that I am not driven to despair, although that word is too strong: in fact, I have no relief in my terrible sorrow, although I have reason to [be sad]. Dear lord, I am letting you know that he who delivered these letters to Your Grace has been given his discharge because of me; the old woman [her mother-in-law] accomplished this with [the help of] the steward who controls the affairs of the kitchen and the cellar and who controls everything, even the lord. He is a traitor and an open criminal, whom no one wanted to hire, except that the lord took him on to please his mother. He [the steward] helps her in all her evil, even her daughters; he even helps her in those affairs I specially wrote Your Grace about the other day in a postscript. He lives with the old woman and with her two daughters, and they are committing a serious evil in the household; but he [Perchta's messenger] will report everything to Your Grace. For he was aware of it and therefore had to be [sent] away because he happily served me and did not want to help them with this matter. That is why the old lady and the same steward denounced him before the lord [her husband]. She did not accuse him openly, but through this steward, and she herself told him [the lord] in secret; then he, as a good servant, took only a good old footman who is now here as a witness, because the lord [her husband] persuaded him [the footman] to stay with him; he is now experiencing living here, but does not intend to stay because he cannot bear to see my wretched way of life. And he [Perchta's messenger] talked to the lord about all the steward's evil doings and everything which he had been ordered to and was supposed to do to me; and I also testified to this good man all that had ever happened to me. So he reported to the lord that a great wrong is being done to

---

[35]   One of her husband's castles in Moravia about eleven kilometers from Mikulov.

me, just as he will well report to Your Grace how this quarrel began and what it is all about. And please believe everything that he will tell you, as though Your Grace had heard it from my own lips, and readily believe me also, because this did not happen secretly. And he declared before the lord and before everyone that had he wanted to help him [the steward] in his crime, and to deceive me, he would not have been dismissed, and that he is being dismissed for no other [reason], but that he was glad to serve me. The lord did not respond to this, but having taken counsel with the steward and his mother, he ordered him to go.

Then all the people raised a clamor against the lord but also against Your Grace, that you can allow me to go through so much. They all shouted at him [Perchta's servant] to go to Your Grace, and, telling me that Your Grace should take action and receive him, and thereby Your Grace can have a clear pretext against him [her husband], [because] he does not keep any of the promises he makes to Your Grace, and that it is a wonder that he can give such favorable reports about me to Your Grace, while doing so much evil around me; saying that it would be fitting to take and burn his [property], and that such a great disgrace and public distress, [known] throughout Moravia and Austria, cannot be a secret to Your Grace, and [asking], how can you possibly forget me so completely? Given in Valtice.

Perchta of Rožmberk.

Postscript

Dear lord and dear father! As one who is powerful and has influence with him [her husband], remember me, my disgrace, my poverty, remember this destitute woman, your child, and do not allow this to happen to me. And, Your Grace, do not yourself commit this shame, and do not allow these things, which are humanly impossible for me to bear. For I suffer these things and this danger to my life and to my honor from this miserable mother and from these two sisters, about which it would not be proper for me to write. For you should know that I have become so desperate that if you do not save me from this [situation], I shall bring a complaint against you before the Lord God; and you shall see that I will not suffer this from them any longer. Still I have started nothing, neither would I want to do anything without your will. I ask for the sake of God, dear lord, please give me your assistance now, for you have forgotten about me as though I have never been anything to you for I am already very grieved at your forgetting me. And God knows that I am without fault in what is happening to me, that in me he has a faithful wife; but he does not make me feel this by any kind gesture. Though I myself write this about myself, I trust God that He grant that you do not find me changed. But he betrays himself to the whole world by the thoroughly disorderly life he lives. And dear lord! I beseech Your Grace with great hope; please do not refuse it for my good. Please receive this servant who has experienced such a wrong on my behalf; I can readily promise for him that he conducts himself like a good and faithful servant. If you would please have him as the steward of the wine cellar or of the beer, even of your own room or of anything you like, [you will find him] a true and skillful servant in all things. He was in the service of Lord Puchomér[36] for five years, and he would like to have him again, but when this happened to him on my account, then it seemed to him, and to me and to others that he [the servant] should go to Your Grace. Since absolutely no one, except I, knows about this, that he has gone to you, please deal with these letters secretly, so that it does not become known that I sent a message through him, but please do not keep it a secret that you have received him for my sake; if Your Grace did not receive [him], and his return here made that fact known, then his life would not be safe, and Your Grace would make me very grieved because of it. For you should know that through this, the people thought[37] that much good would come to me. I can also happily write this to Your Grace as the reliable truth, that it so happened, and please have no fear that I have misled Your Grace. I ask Your Grace to please send me someone whom you trust well, without delay. Instruct him to make inquiries; if he sees things differently, or if upon inquiry it is not as I have made known, please reprimand me promptly. If Your Grace receives him, it will spread among the people; they will know that what is happening to me is not a secret, and if Your Grace does not then take action against the lord, it will only serve to confirm his position. But please also remember that there was a servant of Your Grace in Vienna, and he heard what was happening to him [her servant] on my account. And he [her servant] met the servant who had come from Your Grace, and he instructed him to go up with him, and so it happened that Your Grace received him. I discussed with Stephen[38]

---

[36] George of Puchheim was the butler in the imperial Austrian court. *Listář a listinář*, 4, p. 345.

[37] Lit. much good is supposed to happen to me before the people. Perchta uses the present tense, but her next sentence indicates she refers to something in the past.

[38] A Rožmberk servant.

whether the lord [her husband] would want to proceed against me if it reached Your Grace's ear, how he showed me dislike and slandered me and you, and that he does not keep any of his promises, and that it is now so very burdensome for me, that I do not now want to let Your Grace know about it, because perhaps Your Grace might not believe me because of the great obligation which he has undertaken.[39] Instead, I want to leave it because I know that it will be brought to Your Grace's attention by other people, and [I know] that Your Grace always has someone not far from us who continuously asks about my life, that Your Grace hears more about this from others than he does from me; so I spoke to him. Dear lord, speak to him in this way as well, speak so that my words will agree with Your Grace's speech. O dear lord! if you do not remember me, you will act unjustly to me, and I will die shamefully. Already no one wants to stay with me because of the great disorder and poverty. When you gave me in marriage, it would have been better had you buried me in the ground. For God's sake do not delay in sending someone reasonable to him and let all men promptly ask him to send me to you. And to take a hard stand in this, if he should not want to do so; indeed, you would then have to take a harsher stand towards him, so that he fears you and so that he does not treat me so badly. For he cannot have too many accounts of how nice you are to him.[40]

17.   *Perchta of Rožmberk to her brother Henry reporting on the marriage plans of her husband's brother and her fears that the new bride will side with her in-laws, and that all her own servants may be dismissed. She asks him to come to her and bring her pillows for her personal comfort.*

13 July 1451, Mikulov
Czech   *A Č* no. 26

To my dear brother, the noble lord, Lord Henry of Rožmberk.

I send you my prayers, my noble lord and dear brother! It would make me happy to know that you are well. Dear brother, I am letting you know that my lord [her husband] [is] still in Vienna, and his

---

[39] If her marriage is as Perchta describes it, she believes her father is obliged to intervene. An intervention into the household of another baron, even if he was a son-in-law, wasn't taken lightly. Perchta's following words indicate that her father may not yet have decided upon any action.

[40] Her husband, Lichtenštejn, uses it against Perchta, when her father treats him kindly.

brother Lord Henry is there with him; and someone from Vienna let me know and has written to tell me that, certainly Lord Henry is there because he still wants to get married, and does not want to be much longer without a wife. It [the marriage] may fall apart simply because they do not want to give him the woman he wants. Lastly, he intends to take over Steiregg;[41] I was told [in the letter] to give some thought about what would happen to my dowry, if the Lord God allowed something to happen to me and he took over the castle. But if it was not so, and if his bride would take the side of those [mother-in-law and sisters-in-law] who are now here with me, I should know that, where even now my affairs go badly, he [author of the letter] expects that things will get even worse, since I have no help from either husband or kin; they [her husband's kin] understand this; if it would happen in this way. I am afraid that even my own kin will not be able to help me and that he [her Vienna informant] understands that if this happens, he fears that even my kin will not be able to help me. And he heard that my lord said he will send my servants away, and that he would like to dispose of my servants entirely, so I might never again be able to send [anything] to my kinsfolk and be able to let them know anything. He [her informant] wants me to be happy enough having something to drink and to eat; and so he advises me to let you know this without delay. And he just wrote to me, exactly as I am now writing it. I ask you dear brother, think about this; how I, an orphaned woman, am to live in this world under these conditions. Already my living conditions have been proclaimed everywhere, and everyone talks about it in such a way as though you do not care about me even if I could take care of myself, [but] even a page would not allow this to happen to his child should he be able to help him as you are able. Although it is I who am writing about myself, that I am not guilty towards him [her husband] in any way, I trust God that you will not see it otherwise. But unfortunately you think about me and my situation very little, and always allow delays until it has gone too far. And I have written and sent out so much, but it has helped me not at all, except that I had to suffer more. I beg you dear brother, for the sake of the great faith I have in you, have sympathy towards me and by any means come yourself to [see] me as quickly as you possibly can. If you are already on the road or in Prague, as soon as you return [home] again, I beg you, do not delay and by any means come, since I await you

---

[41] Her dowry castle.

with great longing, constantly fearing that you will not come. And my relations with him are already such that for a long time I have not spoken with him about things that happen to me, or some need I have which might cost a penny. I behave towards him as nicely as possible; but to him, nothing counts, except that it always gets worse; and from that mother, God knows, I also suffer enough evil. It seems to me that so many different things are happening to me, that even a wiser man would have enough to do, should only one of them happen to him. Dear brother, I ask you! Give me a feather quilt, a pillow, and a small carpet, so that when I sit in the wagon, at least I have something to sit on. I trust that you will not hold this against me, that I ask you for these things; in fact, I hope that you can give them to me yourself. And hopefully without any harm to you. And when you yourself have come to me with a wagon, [I hope] you will have brought these things with you. Also let me know which answer my lord gave you through Wolf. Given in Mikulov on Tuesday, feast of St. Margaret [13 July].
Perchta of Rožmberk.

18. *Šiermarka, a lady in waiting in Perchta's court, confirms to Perchta's brother Henry what his sister has written. She rebukes Henry for his indifference, says that Lichtenštejn beats Perchta and that even a peasant woman expects better. She warns that her own brother may come and fetch her.*

13 July 1451 Mikulov
Czech   **A Č no. 27**

Let this letter be given to the noble lord, Lord Henry of Rožmberk.

I send you my prayers, Your Grace, dear lord! I would be glad to hear that the lord is well, but unfortunately, we are not well. I now send Your Grace a shirt; I ask you please to wear it for my sake. But this is why I am angry with Your Grace, and I think that when we see each other I shall argue with Your Grace to the point of tears, for I would never have expected that you would forget your sister as well as us for so long, having promised to come to us, if we were worse off! And now things go so badly for the lady [Perchta], that it is hard for us to look on, as it is for everyone who sees her in this [situation], and still Your Grace does not come to her. People are already talking a great deal about this. She complains to herself about it so much, and she says to me that often she is so depressed that she finds absolutely no hope for herself in anybody, especially when she recalls

Your Grace and laments the fact that she at one time loved Your Grace too much,[42] [and now] it seems to her that Your Grace is already forgetting about her. Often she weeps disconsolately, thinking about this. I am happy to try to talk her out of it whenever I can, but it seems even to me that she is always happy to suffer many upsets,[43] which, as I live, I would never have expected from her. Others say that if it had been a peasant woman that he married, she would not have suffered this much from him; and the more accommodating she is, the worse he and his mother are. She told me that she wanted to ask Your Grace for a pillow and a feather quilt. Dear lord, please give them to her, or you will have to pay for her soul's salvation when she dies, for the old woman does not want to lend her one feather. Also dear lord, please advise me what I am supposed to do about the lord wanting to send us away; I suspect, should my brother know this, for it is no secret anymore as they talk of it everywhere, that her situation is so bad that he already beats her, and that it is only because of us that he dare not and this is why he wants to send us away, so that afterwards he would be able to do what he wants with her; this is what people everywhere in Vienna are already saying. I fear that if my brother knows this he will want to take me away himself. What shall I do? He would have taken me away earlier because of their meanness, had the lady [Perchta] not requested him not to. Dear lord! Your Grace, listen: [my brother] knows well, that I could, may God grant, have an honorable place to call my home, but I myself, because of the devotion I have towards her, do not want to leave her: whatever I could honorably do, I would gladly suffer any affliction, including death. It is so hard for me to watch what is happening to her, that no one can believe me: I trust Your Grace, dear Lord Henry, that you will look kindly on us all, so that we might not become objects of any slander from him, because she remonstrates with herself very much, [saying that] perhaps this person [Lichtenštejn] and this old woman are not even human. Dear lord! We all beseech you, after you return from Prague, please come without delay and think about this, [even] if you have something [else] to do. Do not continue to neglect this matter because of that; for her situation will never improve, unless you come.

Dated in Mikulov on Tuesday the day of St. Margaret [13 July]. Šiermarka.

---

[42] She uses the present tense but referred to a past time. Lit. 'she at one time loves Your Grace too much'.

[43] Lit. strange events.

19. *Perchta of Rožmberk, writing to her brother Henry, mentions her new-born baby, laments her husband's continued indifference and asks Henry to come, adding that she has no money.*

16 July 1451, no place
Czech   *AČ* no. 28

Dear brother, As I wrote that my lord [Lichtenštejn] was still in Vienna, therefore you should know, dear brother, that he came home on Tuesday, on St. Margaret's Day; and that he brought [his] sister here, who is still out of her mind; and here I have this joy[44] in their midst, yet I regret that I am still alive because he himself does not speak nor talk to me reasonably. And my child has to be among them even with this demented maiden, and God knows how long this will go on for him. And this disgraceful mother, who may not even be human, how much evil she does to me! I have to put up with it; it is a wonder that my heart remains in me. Dear brother! For God's sake, come now, I ask you as though [I were] on death's battlefield. I would so gladly see you; it is already too difficult for me to send you letters because I have no money. Therefore dear brother, think about this, so that when you come you might put an end [to all these matters] for me.
No signature

20. *Perchta of Rožmberk asks her brother Henry for her dowry letter because she thinks her brother-in-law is deceiving his wife, who does not have her own letter. She concludes by asking him to bring her some dresses.*

1451, no place
Czech   *AČ* no. 31

To the noble lord, Lord Henry of Rožmberk, my dear brother.

Dear brother! If you find it possible, and if you come, bring the letter which was prepared for me for the dowry with you; because I think it would be a good idea to have the letter read before their older servants and before one other good person. When [you] come, then I would tell you who I mean, if you agree, so that they would be there when you give the dowry to him, for we need to negotiate with them carefully because they are untrustworthy. For lady Katherine

---

[44] Her new-born child.

has now been with us a long time. She was [the bride] for lord Christopher, who did not want to release her because she did not have her letter with her and who, together with his mother, wanted to deceive her – and he did not act justly. Dear brother! That is why I write this, although I am as close to death as they are, but because of these living conditions, with which the Lord God has afflicted me through them, I need to deal with it. Given etc.

And for God's sake, come, while I still have some dresses. Soon I will have almost none because I do not have the means to buy myself any. Would it be possible for you to buy me dresses?
Perchta of Rožmberk.

21.   *Perchta of Rožmberk to her brother Henry about her difficulties in getting permission from her husband, Lichtenštejn, to join her family in Český Krumlov for her sister Lidmila's wedding. She blames her mother-in-law and describes the suggestions Šek, a Lichtenštejn official, made for her trip.*

16 December 1451, Mikulov
Czech   *AČ* **no. 32**

To the noble lord, my dear brother, Lord Henry of Rožmberk.

I send my prayers to the noble lord and my dear brother! In true faith, I was glad to hear that you are doing well. As you write to me, that the lord [her husband] politely challenged the things which you told him about me; I was glad to hear this and I hope, dear brother, that you will make a detailed complaint to the lord for continuing to have this attitude; because I overheard that someone criticised him for not letting me go, and that if someone, besides you, would strongly intervene over this, you might yet talk him out [of keeping me here]. Also, do not believe that Lord William[45] is somehow the cause of it, should I not be allowed to go up [to Krumlov], for I have certainly concluded [that this is not true]. But he is preparing himself for something which he cannot do except deceitfully. He wants to be here, but you should know that his mother interferes a great deal in this as well as in the other matter; this makes me very sad, and, although I try, I can never find anything in which she would truly help me. And now on top of this, because she does not expect you to come, although people think it is probable that your coming would be more likely to have an effect on them now than

---

[45]   William of Lichtenštejn, her brother-in-law.

before, for you yourself with your eyes have seen my residence, she recently committed another act of deceit towards me. And I ask you, dear brother, that you yourself speak to the lord about her, as you yourself might understand that she is largely responsible for many things, so that the lord does not think that I should want to make untrue statements about her on my own initiative. And also, I let you know that Šek was here with me, asking me if my situation had improved because of your intercession; he was surprised that you had left me here, and [asked] whether you had spoken to the lord [husband] about my living conditions. I said to him [Šek] that he did not want to release me to you, and that you complained to him about it; that you yourself came for me and that he [husband] did not want to release me despite your request, and that he [you] would gladly honor him, in the same way as he has honored him [you],[46] and I said that you had instructed me to pass this message on. And I understood that Šek was very sad about it. He spoke to the old woman [her mother-in-law] about it and laid it out to them very gravely. She said to him that she has no control over this, that if it were safe, he [Perchta's husband] would gladly do it. And he [Šek] answered her, that he [her husband] could easily find a safe route for her to Krumlov, if he wanted to. And Šek spoke again to me as follows: that he would gladly advise me and help me in everything, but that you should on no account change your mind, and that you should let him [her husband] know, that you are very disgusted that he did not let me go. Also [Šek said], that you did not speak with him about me, but having seen with his very own eyes how it is with me, you are no longer obliged to forgive him, and [need not fear] public rumors or harm to me, because they themselves [her husband and in-laws] understand that you cannot keep it secret from the public. As long as you have the good will to improve it [the situation], especially what you yourself saw with your own eyes, there is good reason to negotiate my going to [my sister's] wedding, for if he [her husband] does not have a strong fear of you, there is a danger that in the near future, he will cheat me. He [Šek] knows that if it comes to this, you will regret that I am still alive in this world; he [Šek] laid out many things about him [her husband] which weigh very heavily on my mind, and he tells me these things because he would regret it if they should ever happen to me. He also told me that if you cannot otherwise get me out through negotiations, you

---

[46] Perchta literally repeats her conversation with Šek and hence uses the third person 'he' meaning the second person, 'you'.

should take me on the road,[47] although in no way should he give advice against his own lord; if he should see you [personally], he would want to let you know, and this would not harm him, because he [Lichtenštejn] is his lord. So to spare me worries he did not want to tell me any more about how he understands their destructiveness and his unchristian intentions. I also hear that Lord Henry [Lichtenštejn] finally wants to assume control over Steiregg. So, dear brother, I entrust these things first to dear God, and then to you, and I hope above all that, knowing these things, you will not desert me, [but do] what seems best to you. And Šiermarka lets you know that [you] should come again, so that for several weeks in advance we might [prepare] and have dinner again on the occasion of your visit. For we have not dined enough since you left. With this I commend you to God. Given in Mikulov, the fourth day of the week after St. Lucia [13 December].

Perchta of Rožmberk.

22.   *Anéžka of Rožmberk writes to lord Gregory of Klaryc, a Rožmberk official, about some problems she has with an unidentified person, hoping her sister will advise him.*

No date, but after December 1451, no place
Czech   Sedláček, *Sborník*

May this be given to the famous squire Gregory of Klaryc, dear to me.

Dear Gregory! I do not know what to make of this.[48] May the dear Lord [Christ] and his dear mother give him the [right] mind so that he can change, if Lady Švamberk[49] will advise him about it and if he will be with you and will obey; I would still be pleased, and if he will not obey this man, whom you know well, then there would still be great hope. But if he follows this man and he parts company with you, then I do not see any good in it. Let it be committed to the dear Lord God. And I thank you very much and ask You to thank tremendously my dear lord my daddy that he might please not forget me.

Anéžka of Rožmberk.

---

[47] Lit. take me on a pilgrimage.
[48] Lit. I do not know what to praise nor what to see.
[49] Anéžka's sister Lidmila who married Švamberk in late 1451. See Letters 21 and 23.

23. *Ulrich of Rožmberk writes to John of Lichtenštejn explaining Perchta's lengthy absence, mildly disapproving of Lichtenštejn's impatience but indicating his willingness to oblige Lichtenštejn's wishes.*

22 February 1452, Český Krumlov
German   *Listář a listinář*, **4, p. 332**

Noble lord and dear son-in-law, first my friendly service. As I let you know earlier, I requested that you should not hold it against your wife, my dear daughter Lady Perchta, that I have kept her here for the merriment[50] and celebration of the wedding of my dear daughter, Lady Lidmila, her sister. However, I gather from your letter, from how you have behaved towards your wife, that you perhaps have taken offense because I kept her here so long. I ask you not to hold it against her if I [wait] to prepare her for going home until my son Henry gets home. Also you refer to other things in your letter; how your servants are supposed to have taken offense with your wife, my dear daughter...[51] as you in your letter will receive better. I have spoken with your servants and was happy to see that they would have stayed. Then I learned from them that they did not want to stay because they had your business [to attend to] and had to ride home again, and when I learned that they had to ride home again, it did not seem right to me that I should keep them any longer because of your business. It also strikes me [as strange], after all these approaching discussions, that you should send for your wife and my dear daughter with another ten horses. She would have come [home] as to her father, and I did not want her to go beyond your wishes in any matter at all. I ask your favorable reply to this. Given in Krumlov on Carnival day [22 February] 1452.
Ulricus von Rosenbergk.

---

[50] *Freuden.*
[51] A gap in MS makes the meaning of the words that follow obscure.

24.   *Perchta of Rožmberk writes to her brother Henry about the debts she incurred during her pregnancy, her fear of angering her husband and about village gossip which blames her for a new tax. She asks for her dowry payment and warns Henry against meeting with her husband's family in Linz, Austria, before he hears her views on the matters under discussion.*

1453, no date, no place
Czech   *AČ* no. 36

Dear brother! Once again I ask you, for God's sake remember me and send me the money, so that I can deal with my debts. I am reminding you about it again because I had let you know about it earlier; but you know, may God grant it, that I owe 1,800 groschen which I borrowed before my lying-in period, and later [I borrowed] 1,800 groschen more. So it is fair that you should hear about what I spent [the money on]. And from him [her husband] I never get anything. He promised to give me the money, but did not give me any of it, and I know this: if he should give me anything, that it would only be to show me up, because I will not be able to have anything done for myself for such a small sum. I cannot reprove him too much, so as not to make him angry. He might not get angry, but I know that he will always make me promises and that nothing will come of them. And now he has levied a big tax on the people here in the town, and the people want me to pay them what I owe them, which is more than I can do. And I am written down in the taverns and in butchers' shops as some beggar woman, and I feel ashamed that I have to cheat those to whom I am indebted. Indeed, I am very sorry that I have to remind you in this way, and I notice that you did not have pity on me for so long. My dear brother! Remember that love, which, as you know well, I had and still have for you above all other living people...[52] [and which I hope you have for] me already; tell me that you do not want to abandon me, the time is here to show me this, because there is a great need for it. Please know that just now I am sending a messenger to you, and I have not even one penny, nor do I know where I might provide myself with money. Therefore do not delay, and send me the money as soon as possible. And I ask you especially not to delay in sending him the 3,000 groschen; but those due on the Feast of St. Gall [16 October] perhaps could be given to me, when I go up to [Krumlov].[53] And

---

[52] A gap in MS.
[53] The first recorded payment on her dowry was made in late 1452. *AČ*, 11, 261.

whatever you can do to help him, should he ask you, please do not miss the opportunity to do it, so that you prepare him [to agree] to your will. I heard that you may have met in Linz with his brother, and that the reunion was very friendly; you should know that he [Lichtenštejn's brother] greatly fears you because of Steiregg, and that he wants to invite my lord [husband] and me up to Krumlov soon and he himself intends to pay you a visit there. I would be very unhappy about that, should it happen before I arrive [in Krumlov], because I know that there will be plenty of talk and promises from them; I am afraid you will get into a friendly discussion with them and believe them too much. Therefore, if I see you then, and if I report some things to you, this might change your attitude, and, as it would happen after you hear what I have to say to you, it would be very clear that this [information] comes from me. And if you should meet with his brother, take it as a good thing that he tries to make things well between us. In this respect, I ask you especially to tell him [her brother-in-law] that the evil he has done to me makes you very sad, and if he does not want to put this right, that you will not easily forgive him. In this you do me a great favor. Let the person you send to him with the money be knowledgeable, so that I might be able to take counsel with him. For God's sake do not delay in this matter, and arrange to send someone without delay to him and to me. And please order the messenger to be paid.

25. *Perchta of Rožmberk writes to a local member of the gentry, John Rús of Čemin, who is in her family's service with the task of handling her affairs. She urges him to hurry and writes that her recent childbirth caused harm to her health.*

1453, Valtice
Czech   *AČ* no. 37

Let this letter be given to the famous knight, Rús of Čemin.

Perchta of Rožmberk. My prayers I send dear Rús! Oh dear Rús, I ask you for the sake of God and because of my great abandonment and destitution, in which I exist along with the children, do not forget me in your intercession before our lord father and brothers. May they take action so that I be allowed to go up [to Krumlov]; for I have already sunk to such a disastrous state that if I do not go up [to Krumlov] soon, God knows what will happen to me. But I am very alarmed at my brother's trip to Prague, in case it delays [her own trip]; I ask you to remind my brother that he might first arrange this, before he departs. In addition, I must complain of this, dear

Rús, that I have now given birth, and was lying in childbed, which [resulted] in great harm to my health, which [harm] I shall have as long I live; should God allow me to be healthy enough to see you, I will tell you more about it, and you will be amazed that I am alive. And I believe you as my good friend will be upset about this, and ask my brother to show you his letters; I have often written to him at length. Offer my great services to lady Anna and to her daughters. Given in Valtice.

26.   *Perchta of Rožmberk admonishes her brother Henry in the name of the Virgin Mary to act to improve her wretched living conditions, which now affect her children as well. She again blames her mother-in-law for her troubles. In two postscripts she asks to be supplied with a second wagon for travel and expresses gratitude for her secretary and Šiermarka, a lady-in-waiting. She complains about her sister-in-law's way of life.*

August 1453, no place
Czech   *AČ* **no. 40**

To be given to the noble lord, Lord Henry of Rožmberk, my dear brother.

Oh, dear brother, you write to me, [asking] that I send Janek;[54] I have done this as well. You write that you did not intend to forget the matter which I entrusted [to you]: I ask you for the sake of God and for the sake of his mother, for she too was of the female sex, and I admonish you through her holy name, that even if you do not remember that I am a sister to you, then at least remember her [Mary], through whom I hereby admonish you, although I do not do so gladly; I am reminding you in this way. But God knows that I, an abandoned and aggrieved pauper on this earth, do not know what to do now, neither do I know how to write [to you], in order not to become as stiff as wood before I come up to you, so that I might feel neither cold nor hunger, and so that I need not be afraid for these abandoned children, whom the Lord God gave me in my great abandonment, and in order to be able to suffer all of this silently, always gladly wanting to persevere, so that they [her in-laws] would find no blame in me; for in the past I suffered on my own account, but now I also suffer as many woes in my heart for the sake of the children, as for my own sake. At least before we had some place to live, but

---

54 A servant of Perchta.

now, as I have already said, we all indeed have no place to hide our heads. So remember me, dear brother, because of my great love and hope which I have in you, and also because in no way would I like to provoke your indignation; I ask nothing else but that you help me up [to the castle], and as quickly as possible, for already you have unfortunately neglected this matter too much, resulting in evil. For myself, as much as I can, I would rather not let them know how difficult it is for me, because the more they knew how wretched I am, the slower they would be to leave me; and you should know this well, they themselves know well that they do evil to me. The mother, especially, understands how miserably the children are provided for and that they have nowhere to stay. And this happens because of her and because of her daughter, this evil bag[55] and I am not allowed to say anything on any subject, and she knows well that this greatly saddens me, and that I am in her power and can say nothing about it; should I say something, it would do no good for she would scream out at me, and I would in [my] grief and loss of self-control ...[56] [have] said something to her, which I would not like to do. I have never done it, and yet I know they would be glad to find fault with me in whatever manner they could. And I will be very sorry for you if it comes to this, but if I am not soon with you, you will see it [happen]; I shall not avoid it with such a living situation as I have, for none of the young men whom he [her husband] has with him, can bear it. They want to go away because of the disorder and because of hunger, and because they cannot get any payment from him.

Perchta of Rožmberk.

Postscript

And I strongly beseech you, dear brother, that you do not write to him [Lichtenštejn] about me, for I would only suffer because of it, and nothing would come of it; but, when you with the help of God return from your wedding, I ask you not to delay sending someone to him, who could ask him on your behalf to come up to you, so that you yourselves could speak up on my behalf. Let your wife ask for this as well, so that he dare not refuse you, and immediately send one of your servants down with him so that he could help me to prepare better, because I know that they will not readily give me a second wagon. And if I don't have a second wagon, I will not be able to take anything, except what we are wearing, and that would

---

[55] Lit. this evil hide.
[56] A gap in the text.

not be good; so you should know, if you don't send someone, that I would not manage to get it from him and I would not dare to rebuke him. And if it should seem good to you to send lord Puchoméř[57] with him [her husband], you could tell him [Puchoméř], to also send someone for my own needs, so that there will be someone to ride with me. Because my heart greatly fears that if this is not arranged before you ride to Prague, there will be a long delay, and father does not care much about it; and I should also be very glad, if you [and your father] would place a condition on him that the present dowry rent will not be given to him until I am up there [in the castle]. Dear brother, I have written to you now and earlier extensively enough. I ask you, because of your wedding celebrations, do not forget to act on these things without delay, because if much evil befalls me, I will not be able to write then because it is very cold already. Also, as long as I have my Henry,[58] I will be able to write to you. But should the Lord God help me [to get] to you, I would gladly release him and do him some good, as one who serves me faithfully in my writing and in other things in my destitution, as you yourself well understand; I am afraid that he [husband] might dismiss him before I have ridden up [to the castle], although I have not heard anything, yet I fear his evil in this. Dear brother, as long as I have my servants with me, my situation is better, and I can gladly write that they work hard and faithfully with me in my destitution; and for myself, I consider them nothing else but friends and kin. They have all sent their sorrowful prayers and they ask you not to abandon me nor them, but rather help us up to the castle. I am also letting you know that I definitely heard that this evil daughter of ours [her sister-in-law] is said to live immorally again [with somebody] as before, although no such man is here in the castle; but you yourself know well that such a woman can love only a scoundrel, and such as these have freedom with her; I regret for my own sake and for my maidens, that there has to be such misconduct here, where we are. And you should know that they [the maidens] complain very much about it, as do their relatives. I ask you not to send any more messengers by foot, until I have ridden to you, because I fear that they [husband and mother-in-law] might infer that I intend to answer the letters; but if you do not think it [advisable] to do what I ask here, let me know by rider, who can tell me in person.

---

[57] George of Puchheim, a butler in the imperial Austrian court.
[58] Her secretary.

Second postscript

And I ask you, dear brother, if you know [whether you intend to send a rider], let me know in how many weeks he could come, and give me an answer as soon as possible, because I have instructed my messenger to wait in Krumlov. And Šiermarka[59] told me that she wanted to write in order to know what she should do if her brother wanted to take her away. Dear brother, write to her that she must not allow herself to be taken, that she should answer him that, even if she would like to be taken away, it is her duty to stay until she has made [Perchta's situation] clear to you. But dear brother! I want to thank them [her maidens] all once more, that in true loyalty they do not want to leave me alone in my need. And if you have the time, write them all a letter, so that they will continue to act in my interests as they have done in the past. And I ask you, dear brother, for God's sake, do not allow them [husband and mother-in-law] to send them away; this would make me very sad. Also I am asking about the dowry, for you to give it to him because he talks a lot about it; if it were only for me I would not want to impose upon you, even if I needed it more badly than ever. Dear brother, if someone tells the old lady that they cannot treat me this way any longer, she then says that she does me no harm, and that I brought enough money from father, when I was with you. I am very worried about you, for they tell me that many people are dying in Prague.[60] You could have seen me by now; [you] could make a pilgrimage so that you could come to see me.

27. *Perchta of Rožmberk writes a rare happy letter to her father, Ulrich of Rožmberk, announcing a reconciliation between herself and her husband in which each has undertaken to live honorably and lovingly.*

29 July 1454, Valtice
German   Třeboň, ms

Noble, well-born lord and beloved father. First, I offer my willing and obedient service. I gladly and continuously hope that I and my brothers and sisters should be well. And to God be thanks that things are better for me than they were, and therefore I am letting Your

---

[59] Perchta's lady-in-waiting.

[60] She may be referring to some short-lived noble uprisings which occurred in 1453 in connection with King's Ladislas's entrance into Prague, or to an appearance of the plague about which the sources are otherwise silent.

Grace know that my lord [Lichtenštejn] has spoken to me about the message which you have sent him through Stephen.[61] He intends in all matters to act towards me as a devout man should act, and I have often told him [to his face] that I have sought your help as from my dear father and also from my dear brother. As it has been made well known to you and has been told you by other people, I could not treat him otherwise; it was always made known to you that I yearned for nothing else, as God wills. God has gladdened me with this, that according to the best thing my husband has said, he intends to make an honorable effort to live with me as a devout man ought to. I prefer that we are reconciled to one another because the other people who cherish him desire [the same]. I hope that [instead] of speaking against me, he will [now] behave only as my loving spouse, and I the same as I have promised him; I also want to behave towards him, as his loving spouse. And I hope because you are my loving father, that you too will rejoice in this as I rejoice. And my daughter Elska sent her best service to you. Given in Valtice on Monday after Saint Jacob's day [25 July] 1454.

Perchta, born of Rožmberk, wife of Lord John of Lichtenštejn of Mikulov.

28. *Less than a year later Perchta of Rožmberk writes to her brother Henry that her living conditions have deteriorated again. She describes the important role of two Rožmberk servants, John Rús of Čemin and John Baumgartner, and reports that her relations with her father have improved.*

7 March 1455, Český Krumlov
Czech
A Č no. 44

To be given to the noble lord, Lord Henry of Rožmberk, captain in the Silesian principalities of Wrocław, Svidnice, Javor and others, governor in the Six Cities, my dear brother.

I send you my prayers, noble lord and my dear brother. I would like to know if you are doing well, as I hear you are, thank God, and I heartily wish only that you will return to us soon, for this is my heartfelt desire. Dear brother, as you write to me, may God grant that my affairs will go well, and that you will request [John] Rús for this and will take care of this [matter]: Dear brother! I thank you very heartily and I look forward with great hope to seeing you, and I

---

[61] A Rožmberk servant.

am pleased indeed that you want to have Rús at hand. For when Rús is also present, you will be well able to point to him, saying that he is sent to you from father and from our brothers, and he will also be effective in speaking since he will be able to talk about that which he has seen with his own eyes. The lord [father] and my brother insisted on this, in that they want to send him [Rús] to you without delay. I and our brother also insisted on this, that I should speak a little with the lords; I want to make all my other needs, as well as that on which we will agree here, clear and known through Rús. And thank God, dear brother, things are going well between me and father, for it seems to me that what he has heard from other people about my living conditions has affected him, and that it matters to him more than it did before. Also I know that my lord [husband] is very afraid now that you are dealing with this matter, thinking that there was no way that you wanted to allow it to be negotiated without you. I ask you, dear brother, remember me, abandoned, even for the sake of these children, for you well know that I am completely deserted by my husband as well as are these children. Also, dear brother, I am letting you know that Šiermarka's brother has arranged that she will leave me, which is probably not a secret to you, and I want to approach you hoping for advice through Rús about how we might release her [from employment] pleasantly and honorably, because she well deserves it [for what she has done] for me. I sent her brother a letter [through Paugortnar]; Paugortnar[62] knows what is in it, and I instructed him to tell you. If it seems [advisable] to give the letter to her brother, let it be done; if it should not seem [advisable], at least speak with him; whatever seems [right] to Your Grace. And my sister sends many prayers and asks that you come soon. Given in Krumlov the Friday after the translation of St. Wenceslas [4 March].

Perchta of Rožmberk.

---

[62] John Baumgartner, a Rožmberk servant.

29. *Perchta of Rožmberk to her brother Henry indicating that the brother of her friend and lady-in-waiting, Šiermarka, has sent for her. She asks Henry to provide her with a wedding gift as remuneration for her faithful service.*

13 March 1455, Český Krumlov
Czech   *A Č* **no. 45**

Let this be given to the noble lord, Lord Henry of Rožmberk, captain in the Silesian principalities, of Wrocław, Svidnice, Javor and others, governor in the Six Cities, my dear brother.

I send my prayers etc., noble lord and my dear brother, and I would be glad to know that you are doing well and that you will return to us soon, in good health. I let you know, dear brother, that Šiermarka's brother has sent a page for her with horses, and it did not seem [right] to me to send her off like that, but I could not give her any bridal gift because of my great lack of goods; and I raised this with our father and brother and they gave her brother this answer: they do not want to release her in this way anywhere, especially before Easter time, until you come, as the lord [father] and brother indicate through this messenger. I ask you dear brother not to forget about her, because you know that she suffered a great deal with me, and also she has great hope in you, and I ask you, do what you can for her and do it as quickly as possible. And let me know this through this messenger, so that I might know what to do, if they insist on having her. Also, her brother informed [her] that he has spoken with my husband, about whether he wants to give her a dowry or not; he [her husband] said to him that he has nothing to do with it and there is nothing in it for him. Dear brother! Now I commit my affair to God and to you; do not forget us. Sister sends her prayer. Given in Krumlov Thursday 13 March.
Perchta of Rožmberk.

30. *Ulrich of Rožmberk writes to his son Henry about Perchta's marriage, expecting smooth relations between spouses and Perchta's obedience. He wants Henry to wait in Vienna for Perchta.*

24 March 1455 Krumlov
Czech   *A Č* **no. 46**

To be given to the noble lord, Lord Henry of Rožmberk, my dear son.

Dear son Henry! I am letting you know that I want to send

Perchta, my daughter and your sister, down by water to Vienna without delay; therefore, dear son, she will be committed to God and to you. And speak with lord John [Lichtenštejn] so that things go smoothly between them as between spouses, we also want to act towards him as towards a friend,[63] so that he takes her home peaceably [and] away from Vienna. And also speak with him, saying that we trust him as a friend, and hope that he keeps and observes what he has agreed on, and that my daughter also, God grant, has to obey, as his wife. And the rest I commit to you, dear son, that you deal with it, as you know best. Wait for her there, for it would be a huge muddle should she not find you there, for she would have no refuge with anyone, in order to bring these matters to a conclusion. And also, dear son, as I wrote to you earlier asking about the pearls, if it should be possible to buy one *lot*,[64] which has been examined, for twelve florins, then you should buy me one *lot*, if you have the money; if you do not have the money, then do not buy them. Given in Krumlov, on the second day of the week 24 March 1455.
Ulrich of Rožmberk.

31. *Anéžka of Rožmberk writes to her youngest brother John, possibly referring to meting out strong action against Perchta's husband, and reminds her brother to remember the symbol of piety, the crucifix.*

Mid-March, year unknown[65]
Czech   Sedláček, *Sborník*

May this be given to the noble lord, Lord John of Rožmberk, my dear brother.

My dear brother, the noble lord. My hopeful prayer I present to Your Grace, and I would be heartily glad if Your Grace were well and Your Grace's affairs were going according to Your will. And my dear little page! Please think about this, if you can somehow create fear so that what needs to be meted out, might be meted out, because I hear that they are very alarmed and afraid of Your Grace. And my dear little Johnny, my only pleasure is in expecting to see you soon if God grants it. And always have your little crucifix near you whenever you have to do something. May you be commended

---

[63] The original, *přieteli*. The word denoted both friend and kin.
[64] A *lot* was a measure of weight about 17 grams.
[65] Possibly after the death of her brother Henry in 1457, after which John, the eldest brother, in his twenties, assumed control of the estate with his father.

to the dear Lord God. Given on Thursday after the feast of St. Gregory [12 March].
Anéžka of Rožmberk.

32. *George of Kravař, a Moravian kinsman of the Rožmberks, writes to John of Rožmberk telling him that Perchta's situation is urgent and that he is prepared to let her stay with him in his castle at Strážnice.*

13 March 1459, Strážnice
Czech   *AČ* no. 56.

To the noble Lord John of Rožmberk, my especially dear brother.

I present you my service, noble lord and brother most dear! As you know, when we were in Olomouc earlier, we spoke together about the matters affecting Lady Perchta, our sister, which we also brought to [the attention of] his royal majesty.[66] For this reason, I now send you the letters from which you will understand her situation. Therefore, I ask that you do not delay, for God's sake, take care of it; if you do not deliver her dowry very soon her situation will really be serious. If you can, please write to Lord John [of Lichtenštejn] to allow her to come to me and let her stay with me, because he intends to go to Rome soon; for I would gladly have her with me for your sake and would want to offer her honorable sustenance. If you do not agree with this, then make better arrangements for her. For [her] welfare and health, please do not delay. Given in Strážnice on 13 March 1459 the third day of the week.
George of Kravař and of Strážnice.

33. *John of Rožmberk, Captain in Silesia writes the master of the fishpond,[67] a member of the lesser nobility, Příbík of Račov, instructing him to provide Anéžka with some fish.*

10 October 1459
Czech   **Sedláček, *Sborník***

To the famous Příbík of Račov, master of the fishpond, our faithful beloved lord. John of Rožmberk, captain in Silesia: Dear Příbík! I

---

[66] George of Poděbrady. Olomouc had accepted Podbrady as king on 5 July 1458. Frederick G. Heymann, *George of Bohemia: King of the Heretics* (Princeton: Princeton University Press, 1965), p. 176.

[67] The Rožmberks were in the fifteenth century engaged in a vigorous effort in building fishponds and damming streams to produce fish for the market.

request that you give the maiden Anéžka our sister, in Třeboň, four casks of fish as well as ten pike, six smaller ones and four larger ones. This is all that we require. Given on 10 October 1459.

34. *Perchta of Rožmberk writes to her brother John with joy. She writes that negotiations for delivery of the dowry are in progress and that her husband treats her pleasantly. She asks her brother to cooperate with him as her husband faces conflict with his own family. Because her Czech-speaking secretary has left, she recruited a German writer.*

1459–60, no place
Czech *AČ* **no. 59**

To be given to the noble lord, Lord John of Rožmberk, my dear brother.

I send you my service, noble lord and my dear brother! From the bottom of my heart I would like to see that you are well; because of God's help things go well for me also, for my situation is much better than before. I ask you, as my dear brother, for the same thing which my husband asked you for [through] Špán,[68] and as he now writes, [asking] that you accept him as a friend in this matter; in this do not doubt that he is sincere. For all this, I ask only that you do not give my dowry to him too soon. I promised him that I would ask you for it, but do not do it. I finally understand that he wants to act on all these matters with your counsel. I also understand that he sent such a message to you in great hope and trust in you. Also, he requested that I ask you for this [support]. You should know that not one of all his brothers trusts him, and he has no support from them and stands in great fear of them, and he wants to give himself totally [to work] with you. Dear brother! Since the Lord God, out of his mercy, turned his purpose, his kind heart and his faithfulness towards me, which I otherwise do not understand, I beg you as my dear brother, not to oppose him [her husband] in anything that he asks of you; for in this way you will convert him fully to yourself; and if you do this, and act in a friendly manner towards him I will be in a greatly improved situation, and even better. Had he not spoken with you in Brno so amiably, it would go badly for him with his brother, and he knows this himself. They treat him as though they wanted to force him to do their will, especially his mother's bastard son. A German secretary who does not

---

[68] Špán of Barštejn and of Záhoří was an official with the Rožmberks.

speak any Czech is writing this letter. And my husband had sent [a message] to Mikulov ...[69] to her bastard son, because he [the son] is the burgrave[70] there, [saying] that they might loan him [her husband] some money, and he wants to write to you, that they did not want to loan ...[71] that he lives pleasantly with me, and that they would gladly disrupt it if they could. I would not write this to you but my husband became very angry because of it, and ordered me to write this to you, as from myself, pointing out that he has to suffer great scandal on my account. I told him that I would not write this willingly; and he said that with God's help, he wants to trust you more than he has; therefore you have to believe that he trusts [you]. I beg you to give him a very friendly response to his letter, and show him your concern about the money. You will give him great pleasure, and do not have any worries about redeeming [the loan]; let us know when you have arranged it properly and send Špán to us with it [the arrangement], and do not delay with it. When Špán comes, I will let you know how God and the mother of God take pleasure from our love. I beg you, by all means, send Špán to us for my welfare. And dear brother, I ask you for God's sake, do not let anything be put in his way, as far as you can, so that our friendship is not destroyed. And he said to me that if it pleases you, he wants to ride to you together with me, but he did not order me to write this. Dear brother! Send us some dried trout, for my husband sincerely asked me for it, and treat this his messenger well, and believe what he will speak to you about. Dear brother! I have often written with great sorrow, but this letter [is written] with great joy. Perchta of Rožmberk.

Postscript

Dear brother! If the brothers of my husband acted wrongly against him, I beg you as my dear brother, to be a counsel and helper to him, as he hopes in you. If our dear brother, the priest bishop [Jošt] of Wrocław, [is there], let him know our prayers, and that we would have written to him had we known for sure that he was [there]; and ask him to show the same goodwill to my husband, for my welfare, just as I ask you to. I beg you with great faith, do not dismiss this messenger without a gift, for it is my lord's hope that because of this good news, which he brings from us, you will be very happy and will not leave him without a gift. Do not spread his

---

[69] Gap in text.
[70] The governor in a castle, next in authority to its owner.
[71] Gap in text.

good intentions widely, in case he should change, for his mother strives to disrupt things between us.

35. *George of Kravař writes to John of Rožmberk that Perchta stayed with him and that the disputes within the Lichtenštejn family threaten Perchta's security.*

17–22 March 1461, Strážnice
Czech   *AČ* no. 62

To the noble lord, Lord John of Rožmberk, my especially dear lord and brother.

My services etc. Please know that I always with true faith pray that [you] may be well, in health and getting on happily. For, thank the Lord God that I also am as healthy as I am. Moreover you should know that just now lady Perchta, our sister, was with me in Strážnice, and here I understood that some disagreements and arguments have arisen and broken out between Lord John [of Lichtenštejn] and [his brother] lord Henry,[72] through which, if they are not soon brought to a fitting resolution, I fear that much bad could come between them and their people. Therefore, dear lord brother, I beg you, please do something without delay, and, as far as it is up to you, do not delay to make your intervention known, so that these things can be resolved happily without further strife between them. Given in Strážnice.

George of Kravař and of Strážnice.

36. *Jošt of Rožmberk invites his sister, Anéžka of Rožmberk, to visit him.*

10 April 1461, Kutná Hora
Czech   Sedláček, *Sborník*

May this be given to the noble maiden, Maid Anéžka of Rožmberk, our dear sister.

We present our service and brotherly love, noble maiden, dear maiden sister! I ask you to come to see us this next Thursday in Strakonice and travel together with anybody whom you regard as fitting, for we will take care of the provisions. Given in [Kutná] Hora on the first Friday after Easter.

Jošt by God's grace Bishop of Wrocław.

---

[72] Herrych.

37. *Anéžka of Rožmberk writes to two Rožmberk officials, John Rús of Čemin and John of Petrovice, requesting a contingent of local knights to ride with her to visit her brother, and asks for some cloth.*

12 April 1461, Třeboň[73]
Czech
                                              Sedláček, *Sborník*

May this be given to the famous squires, our dear John Rús of Čemin and John of Petrovice, burgrave in Krumlov.

Dear Rús and burgrave! I am sending you the letter in which the priest bishop, our dear brother, writes to us that we should ride to him this Thursday in Strakonice, as you will understand from the letter. And therefore I ask you to send us George Sedlecký,[74] along with two or three others, to come here to Třeboň this Wednesday, the earlier the better, and ride with us to Strakonice[75] because we have no one with whom to ride. And I trust that you will not exclude me in this matter; and tell Borovec, who has one measure[76] of red cloth, to send it with this messenger whether [it is] cut or whole. Given in Třeboň the Sunday after Easter 1461.
Anéžka of Rožmberk.

38. *Perchta of Rožmberk's security bond for a loan she made to her husband, John of Lichtenštejn.*

19 December 1463, Strážnice
German
                                              Třeboň, ms

I, Perchta, born of Rožmberk, wife of Lord John of Lichtenštejn of Mikulov, acknowledge that I have given this bond letter, received from my above-named dear husband, valid in today's cities to the amount of 563 gulden [about 20,000 groschen], to my dear brother Lord George of Kravař and of Strážnice to hold in public trust. However, with the following understanding: when the above-named, my dear husband or his heirs, should redeem this bond with the above-named sum of groschen, then my above-named dear brother shall forgive that which has been entrusted without any dispute or anything else.

---

[73] The castle, residence, and estate given to Anéžka, as her share of the family patrimony.
[74] A local member of the gentry in Rožmberk service, as was Borovec.
[75] About seventy kilometers distant.
[76] About sixty centimeters.

Should the situation be such that he does not redeem it and death takes him or that death takes me, which may God prevent, the bond is to be entrusted to no one except Lord Jošt, Bishop of Wrocław, and Lord John of Rožmberk, my dear brothers. And should the heirs of my dear husband want to redeem the bond, then the above-named dear brothers shall give them [the bond] for the above-named sum of groschen, also without dispute and without any objection. With this letter, with my pressed seal as documentation, given in Strážnice on the second day of the week after [the feast] of the virgin Lucia [13 December] 1463.

39. *Perchta of Rožmberk describes to her brother Jošt what she thinks was her husband's unwise business transaction with his brother. In response to his request she loaned him money which she raised by riding from village to village pawning her jewels. She insures herself by sending the documents to her kin for safe-keeping. In a postscript she expresses her appreciation of her husband's company, but reveals that she expects no true love from him and with his consent is preparing an agreement whereby she can leave him. She wants Jošt's advice in this.*

24 or 31 December 1463, Valtice
Czech   *AČ* no. 66

To the high prince and lord, Lord Jošt, bishop of Wrocław and my gracious lord and my dear brother.

Gracious and high prince and gracious lord and my dear brother! I send your princely grace my humble prayers, and I would like to know that Your Grace is doing well and is in good health. I am letting Your Grace know that I thank God for the good health I now have, but I am very unhappy that I never hear that Your Grace intends to visit me in my forsaken state, and, God grant that I have not done anything wrong against Your Grace for which I would deserve to be so forgotten and in such difficult circumstances. More-over, I am letting Your Grace know that my husband unnecessarily mortgaged his best property to his brother, even though he had enough money. But because of his great stubbornness, he did not want to pay with money. So for a little money, he mortgaged the property to his brother; his brother treated him with hostility and wanted to deprive him of it. Should my husband ask from Jews the same amount as his brother had loaned him on that property, it would be easier to get it out of them than out of him, as Your Grace, may God grant, will later learn and hear from my lord; and then, my husband, having made this pledge, was seized by such great grief that he immediately went out of his mind again, just as before. And then he sent for me, saying that he remembered with regret that he had dealt unjustly with me, and that he wants to behave properly towards me, and he asks me to remember how unjustly his brother does business with him, and [asks me] to advise him and help him, so that he might get the property back again, and that he wants to remember this to my advantage. I gave this answer, that I have always waited humbly for this, and with prayers hoped that he would behave differently towards me, and now that he has done so ...[77] I would accept it with great gratitude, and whatever I can do to advise and help him, I want to do gladly, not remembering anything that has happened to me. And so I pawned my jewels, and they loaned me partly gulden and partly bonds for them; and wherever I negotiated, riding [from place to place], thank God, I was graciously received everywhere, by good people. And so I have redeemed the property, and with the counsel of our dear brother Lord George [of Kravař] and of other good people, I requested from my lord the pledge-bonds of that little town, which had been pawned to his brother, so that I might pay the good people according to the terms to which I had committed myself. And these bonds I am sending to Your princely Grace, and here Your Grace will understand that I requested nothing improper, nor did I seek any profit for myself from it, only wishing to save my husband. And this was also his goodwill, and he made out this bond for me and I brought it to his brother, asking him that he [also] make out a bond for me, after I had repaid him the pledge on the little town, and he [the brother] promised to me and my husband that he will be happy to attach his seal to it, and at the same time he said many honorable things to me. But when the time came, he did not want to provide me with the bond, out of pure displeasure because I had helped my husband in this. I had hoped to take from him only the gulden which I owed. He asked me to mortgage again to him that which had earlier been mortgaged to him, and more, and that he wants to give to me enough so that [I] can repay what I owe for my jewels. I did not want to do this against my husband's interests. Then my husband made me another bond without a pledge, and the things are partly paid for and I redeemed the jewels, but of that only 550 gulden [about 19,000 groschen] are yet to be paid. I am sending Your Grace [copies of]

---

[77] Gap in manuscript.

both these documents; that is, the first one that was supposed to be completed and the one which was [in fact] completed and which I brought to Strážnice, to our brother [George of Kravař], for safe-keeping in trust, and added to it a similar document to the one I am sending Your Grace; and Your Grace will understand it all well. And I beseech Your Grace, as my gracious lord and brother, if the Lord God should not keep my husband [alive] until the time by which this has to be paid, that Your Grace with our other dear brother, Lord John, will help me as regards my husband's brother, so that I will be paid, as this document attests. I ask Your princely Grace not to hold it against me that I did not bring this to Your Grace first, before I set up these things. It had to be done without delay. I ask Your Grace to please send this and the other documents to our brother Lord John in Krumlov, to whom I am writing more briefly because he [John] may understand all from this letter. I write this with the counsel and knowledge of our dear brother Lord George [of Kravař], who graciously accepts me [and] all my troubles. I beg you to please thank him for it; he sends this message for me at his cost. I could not arrange it myself, as I am so poor. With this, I commend Your Grace to God. Given in Valtice, on the seventh day of the week before the New Year.

Perchta of Rožmberk.

Postscript

Gracious prince! May Your Grace be pleased to know that now, thanks be to God, I have what I need to eat and to drink, and my husband eats with me and has been with me since the time that I arranged and organized those affairs [for him], and helped him out of even greater difficulties than those about which I wrote to Your Grace, such that it is not fitting to write about them. And before I paid this [money] into his hands, he made me many favorable promises, but when he had it in his hands again, then he showed me less and less of his goodwill, and I find no true love in him, nor is there any hope of it. You should not find this hard to believe, for to him nothing is more dear than money, and he occupies himself with it day and night. I am afraid that in the end no [lasting] good will come of this, but I do not regret, nor do I want to regret, that I showed him faithfulness; the Lord God will be my reward. I should have let Your Grace know this a long time ago, but I was afraid to write this because of him, and it has already overtaken me, for I understood that he began [to show] me this love out of great need; so I do not remind him of this by saying a single word. Gracious prince! I beg Your Grace for God's sake, please do not withdraw yourself from me and please send a message to my lord [husband], earnestly asking that he release me to come to Your Grace. If Your Grace will request this of him with diligence, I know he will not be able to refuse it because it was agreed that I should ride to Your Grace; but, Your Grace, please do not let him know that Your Grace knows about it [the agreement]. And nothing else would prevent it, except that he hesitates to pay for my travel expenses. But I need it very much and it is good for me, because if I do not arrange now what I have decided for myself with the consent of my husband [I will have no other opportunity]. And when Your Grace hears this, then Your Grace will understand that I am striving for nothing else but respect, and later I might not be able to achieve it. In addition to that, our dear brother Lord George [of Kravař], who knows my living conditions and the habits of my husband, advises me to always talk to Your Grace in person, and entrust some very difficult matters to Your Grace, which it would not be right to keep silent about. And he [George] also promised me that he intends to give me an escort, and that, riding out of his home, he will accompany me the length of his property up to Štramberk,[78] and that it will not be necessary for me to spend anything for my sustenance. And knowing this, my gracious lord and brother, I beg Your Grace, please Your Grace, remember me with brotherly love, and show your diligence in this matter, for I request this out of love for dear God, that I might see Your Grace, for it seems to me to have been a very long time since I have seen Your Grace. This message also has the consent of my husband, and in addition I have explained to him that I want to mislead Your Grace, [by saying] that I deposited a document with Lord George, which is supposed to be given to Your Grace, should it be necessary.[79] And he [husband] instructed me to send my documents to Your Grace and to make known as widely as I can how his brother deals with him; he also asked me to ask Your Grace from him, to send him a first-class marten fur coat with a fully prepared collar; he will gladly pay for it immediately and so deserve it from Your Grace, and he wanted to send the gulden immediately now, but feared the dangers; and I greatly beseech Your Grace to please do

---

[78] About 150 kilometers distant from her Moravian residence, Valtice.

[79] In this, and the next letter, Perchta describes in vague terms her settlement with her husband allowing her to leave him without giving up her income from her dowry. The agreement requires a degree of secrecy because she does not mention the words, "departure" or "separation". Her departure and difficulty in collecting her income become evident in subsequent letters.

this for my benefit, and as soon as might be possible. And if Your Grace does it, he will let me go all the sooner. And I also beg Your Grace, if you will please send me four marten pelts; I need them very much. Please reply letting me know what you intend.

40. *Perchta of Rožmberk writes to her brother John expressing her obedience to him and alluding to her preparations to leave her husband's household as she wrote to her brother Jošt, the bishop of Wrocław. She calls her decision to leave a matter of self-respect.*

23 or 31 December 1463, Valtice
Czech   *AČ* **no. 67**

To the noble lord, Lord John of Rožmberk, my dear brother.
    I send you my prayers, noble lord, dear brother! I would like to know that you are doing well and are healthy. I am letting you know that I now have good health, thanks be to God. But I am very dejected because you have not sent anyone to me, and that is what you promised me and wrote to me from Brno. Dear brother! How am I supposed to accept that you take such a hard attitude towards me, that you forget me so, knowing about my desolate existence, while, may God grant, I have not wronged you, nor do I intend to wrong you, with God's help, but I consider it right to behave myself towards you like an obedient sister. I believe, dear brother, that you will think of me differently, for you must surely know that I have a hard and desolate home with my husband, and I have no expectation that it will be changed with him into something different, but [on the contrary] I anticipate something horrible about which it would not be fitting to write. But, dear brother, I beseech you for God's sake, have mercy on me and do not refuse me this; send Špán[80] to me as quickly as you can, and do so for my welfare, for I have resolved to do something, with the knowledge of my husband. I cannot achieve this myself without your counsel and help, nor do I want to act on it without your consent and knowledge. And once you know about it, may God grant, you will understand that I am striving for nothing else but respect; and if I do not arrange it now, I will not be able to later. I believe that you, knowing this, will not delay in arranging for me to meet with you in person. I need this, but I would also like to see you out of love. Also dear brother, you should know that I wrote

---

[80] Špán of Barštejn and of Záhoří was a courtier with the Rožmberks, see above p. 42 n. 26.

the priest bishop [her brother Jošt] at length and he is supposed to send you my documents as well as others, and then you will understand how I am doing. I ask you not to desert me in this matter, concerning that letter which is deposited with lord George [of Kravař] in Strážnice, our dear brother. Given in Valtice, the Saturday before the new year.

41. *John of Rožmberk writes to his sister Perchta of his sadness at the news in her previous letter.*

January 1464, no place
Czech   *A Č* **no. 68**

I send you my service, noble lady and dear sister! I would be happy to know that you are doing well and that things are well, but what you have written to me in great detail saddens me. I let you know that, God willing, we will soon meet with the priest bishop [Jošt], our lord brother; and when we are together, I want to discuss with His Grace all those things about which you have written to me, and we will together, with Lord George [Kravař] of Strážnice, our kinsman, resolve what to do, so that the result is improvement for you and respectability for us. And I have sent a copy of what I am writing to you to George of Strážnice, and now I also enclose a copy of what I am writing to him. I thank [you] very much for the scarf which you sent me, just as [I would thank] my lover.

42. *John of Rožmberk writes to George of Kravař preparing for a meeting with King George of Bohemia and with Perchta's brother Jošt, Bishop of Wrocław, to discuss Perchta's situation.*

Summer of 1464, Český Krumlov
Czech   *A Č* **no. 69**

To the noble lord, Lord George of Kravař and of Strážnice, my especially dear kinsman and brother.[81] My services etc. As you have written to me that we should do something about the lady our sister: I am letting you know now that around the feast of St. Jacob [25 July] and the feast of St. Philip [23 August] both the priest bishop and I will be in Prague, and there we want to speak about these

---

[81] Although both Perchta and John call George of Kravař their brother, he was actually the brother of their grandmother, Eliška of Kravař. See *Listář a listinář*, 4, pp. 395, 438. See also Letter 32.

things with his Royal Grace[82] and to make use of His Grace's counsel as our lord, for we did these things with His Grace's counsel and we summoned our Lichtenštejn brother-in-law on His Grace's advice earlier, as is no secret to you. And whatever His Grace advises us as our lord, we will let you and our sister know without delay so that ... it is, God knows, true that our brother-in-law does not keep [his word] in these things ...[83]

43. George of Kravař informs Perchta's brother John of Rožmberk of the help he has given Perchta, and urges John to act on his sister's behalf because he believes the lives of Perchta and her daughter are in danger.

3 July 1464, Strážnice
Czech *AČ* no. 70

To the noble lord, Lord John of Rožmberk, my especially dear brother. My service etc.

You may remember how many important messages regarding lady Perchta, our sister, I have sent to you, indicating how her situation with her husband is and how badly it stands, how I forwarded her frequent letters to you; not regretting the expense and effort involved, asking you please to take care of things.[84] Once more, you will be able to understand from her letters, which I enclose, that she and her daughter have been placed in danger. Understanding [this from] these [letters], please, if you think it [right] to you, do something about it without delay in case she and her daughter die because of this. For could I do this properly myself, I would be only too glad to do my best. And dear lord brother, I would be glad to learn that you are healthy and that all is well, for I also, thank God, walk now as I am able.[85] Given in Strážnice, the third day of the week before St. Procop's [4 July] 1464.

George of Kravař and of Strážnice.

Postscript

Dear lord brother, I hear that you might have some good young bloodhounds which can be trained; therefore I ask that you might

---

[82] King George of Poděbrady was elected in March 1458, with the support of John of Rožmberk. See Introduction, above, pp. 15–17.

[83] Parts of the MS are illegible.

[84] Kravař illuminates how Perchta's letters made their way to her family home, whether as part of regular communication, or by special messenger, is not clear.

[85] He is referring to either an accident or injury from which he is recovering.

supply me with one suitable for training, so that I might order it to be trained, and so that it might be trained as a tracker. And should God grant you to come to Moravia, and I have some wild game, I shall keep you in mind.

44.   *Jarohněv of Úsuší, the military captain of Anéžka's castle, Třebon, writes to John of Rožmberk that he has given the invitation to Anéžka and now requests a coach for her travel.*

4 December 1464, Třeboň
Czech   Sedláček, *Sborník*

May this be given to the noble lord, Lord John of Rožmberk, my gracious lord. Noble lord, my gracious lord! I have done just as Your and the Lady's Grace [John's wife, Anna Hlohovská] dictated, and asked Her Grace the maid [Anéžka] to come to Your Grace in Manštein[86] this Saturday, and Her Grace agrees to Your and the Lady Grace's request. Therefore please do not delay in sending a coach for Her Grace this Friday as well as two valets on horse; and I, Gregory, also ask that you please do not leave it any longer, since you told me to come, because later I may not be able to come as quickly. Given in Třeboň the third day of the week on the day of St. Barbara, the virgin and martyr [4 December], in the year 1464.
Jarohněv of Úsuší captain in Třeboň.

45.   *Anéžka of Rožmberk sends her brother John some letters received from their sister, Perchta, as well as a deer she has killed.*

31 July 1465, no place
Czech   *AČ* no. 71

May this be given to the noble lord, Lord John of Rožmberk, my dear brother.
Noble lord, my lord and dear brother! I send Your Grace my service, my dear little page; with true faith I yearn for Your Grace and especially for the children. Enclosed I send Your Grace the letters from Lady Perchta. I beg Your Grace to please give an answer as soon as you are able, for the messenger of Lord George [of Kravař] is still waiting here with me. I am not ill at all, after

---

[86]   Majdštejn or Dívčí Hrad was a castle belonging to the Rožmberks.

coming home. And herewith I send Your Grace a deer which I killed myself as I was riding on the road home.
Anéžka of Rožmberk.

46. *Gregory Klaryc, a member of the lesser nobility in Rožmberk service, sends John of Rožmberk a deer killed on the hunt.*

1 August 1465, Třeboň
Czech   Sedláček, *Sborník*

I am sending Your Grace a deer. Yesterday again a good stag and two fawn were killed by the master of the hunt. And the maiden sister of Your Grace directed [me] to write that she is not at all afraid of death, and that she is letting Your Grace know that she killed a deer etc. [Given in] Třeboň, 1 August 1465.

47. *John of Rožmberk reminds John of Lichtenštejn of the prolonged efforts to resolve Perchta's unhappy marriage and suggests that three Austrian noblemen be entrusted to mediate the settlement.*

1465 undated, no place
Czech   *AČ* no. 75

I send you my service, noble friend and dear brother-in-law! You know and are well aware that for a long time, during the life of my lord father and my brother of blessed memory, we spoke and negotiated through messengers on the matter of my sister and your spouse, because of her great destitution, which continues to be unresolved. But [our effort] has produced no effect. God knows, I would be glad if we could be together in friendly association, since we are related. Moreover, I suggest Lord Ekkercavar, Lord Poterdorfer, and Lord Ruger Starhenbergér, or two of them if that is enough, to make peace between us, so that she be properly provided for according to justice. I will be glad to see this [come to pass], the sooner the better. Should you perhaps not want to do this, you should know that I and my kinfolk could not stand by and watch any longer, if she becomes the object of ridicule, shame and poverty, a scandal to her and to us all. I ask for your answer by letter to be returned by this messenger.

48.   *John of Rožmberk to a friend of Lichtenštejn, an unnamed nobleman and a guarantor of the dowry letter, asking him to help in settling the dowry so that Perchta can leave her husband.*

1465, no place
Czech   *AČ* no. 76

I demonstrate to you my service, noble lord and dear friend! You are aware, how for a long time during the life of my lord father and my brother of blessed memory, we have made an effort on behalf of Lady Perchta, our sister, wishing her to be properly looked after according to justice. And you always spoke in a friendly way with the lord [Lichtenštejn]. So now I am writing to him about this. I am sending [you] a copy of this settlement,[87] asking that you speak to him[88] immediately as a friend. And since your seal is also attached to the dowry letter, I trust you as a friend to act, just as my kinsman, Lord Zdeněk, discussed with you a while ago. For you should know, that if nothing comes of it, and he continues to inflict such destitution and poverty upon her as she has borne up to this time, and [which has] been no small shame to himself, to me and to our kinsmen, neither I nor my kinsmen could stand by and watch it any longer. I request your answer by this return messenger.

49.   *Anéžka of Rožmberk writes to her brother John, concerned about his health and that he is going off to war.*

mid-November, year and place unknown
Czech   Sedláček, *Sborník*

May this be given to the noble lord, Lord John of Rožmberk, my dear brother.

Noble lord and my dear lord brother! I offer you my very forlorn prayer, unfortunately having heard the bad news that you are to ride off to war. I would not worry at all if only Your Grace would not go. Also they told me that Your Grace had a very heavy stone at Nový Hrad.[89] My dear little Johnny! I ask Your Grace, please let me know

---

[87] A copy of the settlement has not survived. The addressee of the letter is in a position to persuade Perchta's husband to help her secure her income because the addressee's seal is attached to the dowry document as a guarantor for Lichtenštejn.

[88] Lit. this be done.

[89] Most likely a gallstone. For a description of gallstones by a fourteenth-century professor of anatomy and surgery at the University of Bologna, see Kenneth Kiple, ed., *The Cambridge World History of Human Disease* (Cambridge: Cambridge University Press, 1993), p. 740.

the truth: how you are and, as regards this war, for God's sake, what do you anticipate and would you like a really effective medicine concocted for you? And I am now sending from my own household, some pudding sausage, made from my own pigs which has already been boiled; only please have it baked for you. And I thank you exceedingly, Your Grace, for the partridges, my dear little lord, dear God [only] knows when I will see you [again]. Given in Třeboň the Sunday before [the feast of St.] Othmar [16 November].

Anéžka of Rožmberk.

50. *Perchta of Rožmberk writes to her brother John from her family home, referring to her renewed problems collecting her dowry according to the terms of the agreement she reached with the Lichtenštejns at the time of her departure in 1465.*

1 February 1470, Český Krumlov
Czech   *AČ* **no. 77**

Let this be given to the noble lord, Lord John of Rožmberk, supreme chamberlain of the Bohemian kingdom, my lord and dear brother.

My prayers etc. I understood from your letter and the letter of the priest John [Kaplicer], that you are diligent about me, and for this I am very thankful, [and accept it] as from my dear lord and brother. I continue to present myself in good hope, for you yourself know and understand from whom I have had many promises, and in whom I have placed these hopes. For me, things are now going backwards and I am very sad about this. Do not worry that I might do something unexpected, or that I might do something without your knowledge or consent. I am glad to hear that you are well and have good health. And may the loving God grant happiness. Given from the castle Krumlov on Friday 1 February 1470.

Perchta of Rožmberk.

51.   *Perchta of Rožmberk writes to her brother John who is on his way to see Lichtenštejn. He and a priest in Rožmberk employ are to find ways to effect her 1465 agreement and if possible bring some of her personal effects to Krumlov. She expresses concern over her son who stayed in Mikulov with his father when she left.*

14 February 1470, Český Krumlov
Czech   *AČ* no. 78

To the noble lord, lord John of Rožmberk, my dear brother.I send you my prayers, noble lord and dear brother! I am glad to hear that you have good health and are well and I trust that when you see that the time is right, you will not forget me. And should they continue not to want to come to an agreement, [you should] eventually seek an answer, so that you might consult further with your kin and friends. You ask me, if I wish you to bring with you some of my things; this would make me very happy. I entrusted the priest, John, when he rode away, to speak with my son about the payment and about the bond on my debt, and I sent him the letters containing my request that all which could not be sold should be sent with you. I also wrote to [Balthaser] Auer;[90] the most important items about which he is supposed to speak with my son are listed in [my] letters to him. But from the priest John's [Kaplicer's] letter I understand that he has not spoken with my son about anything, nor did he give the letters to Auer. And my son writes to me, and so does Auer, in response to the letter which I sent to you, that they both agree voluntarily to do everything for me; I am not at all sure what I should do about these matters. But I ask, dear brother, when once this letter finds you, immediately, without delay, summon Auer to come to you and ask him about all these things; I am writing to him not to hide anything from you; he knows everything. If your help is needed, I trust that you will not desert me in this, so that I might come into what is mine. And should my son yield, then do not converse openly with him, lest he becomes alienated from me through this. And whatever you learn about these things which I ought to know, I trust you to summon me; should it seem [to you] that you yourself could negotiate something or write [something] on my behalf, you have my full authority for this; my seal is with the priest John. May God grant that it goes well and successfully, and

---

[90]   A member of the lesser nobility in Rožmberk service. *Listář a listinář*, 4, p. 349.

that [your] wife, thanks be to God, is doing well, as are the children. Given in Krumlov, the fourth day of the week on St. Valentine's Day [14 February] 1470.

52.   *Perchta of Rožmberk, writing to her brother John, reveals that her dowry payments are again a source of trouble for her as the Lichtenštejn family is not paying her. She is concerned about alienating her son, who resides with his paternal kin.*

23 February 1470, Český Krumlov
Czech   *A Č* **no. 79**

To the noble lord, Lord John of Rožmberk, supreme chamberlain of the Czech kingdom, my dear brother. My dear brother! I am glad to hear that you are in good health. And I am very glad to hear that, as you have written to me, [you] have brought my affairs to a conclusion; I am very grateful for your diligent work. And may the Lord God grant me the resolution and ability to conduct myself towards you as is fitting at all times. Remember, dear brother, to make the matter so secure at this time that you will not have any more work to do on this later, for you yourself know these people well; and if you think it [right], insist that on St. George's Day [23 April] half of the annual rent is delivered to me, because I am in great need. Also, I understood from the letter of John the priest that my affairs have not made a good start so far as my son is concerned, and I cannot think of anything better than to commend it to the priest John, giving him full authority to work at it as he was instructed; if he cannot negotiate it himself, let him give it over to you. And I trust you as my dear brother, that you will not abandon me in this, for if the Lord God helps me to succeed, so much and more will come of it than what you have now negotiated. With this may you be commended to the dear God, and may God grant that [you] return to us in health, having negotiated your affairs well. Given in Krumlov on Thursday after the feast of St. Peter [22 February].

53. *Anéžka of Rožmberk writes to Jarohněv of Úsuší, a Rožmberk official and friend, about her travels and her sister Perchta, and mentions some bad news from the family castle, Český Krumlov, which will keep her from their anticipated meeting at the annual fair.*

28 June 1470, Třeboň
Czech   Sedláček, *Sborník*

Let this be given to the noble squire Jarohněv, dear to me!

My dear old man! I want you to know that, thank the dear Lord God and the dear mother of God, I have arrived home, and I was a true knight, because I did not get sick at all; but my sister [Perchta] is still in bed, so I am not able to write on her behalf, nor write about her, but I would rather speak to you about this myself as soon as possible. But even on the way, before I got home, I unfortunately heard news from you from Krumlov which greatly saddened me; and if things are as I heard, I fear that I will not have the opportunity[91] to speak to you very soon, and I do not know how to express myself well in writing. In line with my sister's requests and needs, a response should be given to her regarding certain issues immediately. Should I be able to act quickly, we should be able to get a message there this Sunday at no expense to ourselves. And had I not heard the bad news, I would immediately have ridden to you in Krumlov, so that I could be with you during this year's fair, [but] I do not want to put you to the trouble of travelling in these dangerous times. But unfortunately because of this business I cannot come to you. O dear Jarohněv! As long as there is someone left on this earth,[92] things will go wrong! I commit you to the dear Lord God; may the dear Lord God and his dear mother be your helper and comforter, he who never deserts the just and the righteous. Given in Třeboň on Wednesday after the eighth day of the feast of Corpus Christi.

[91] Lit. have you so soon.
[92] Lit. as long as the earth carries someone.

54. *Anéžka of Rožmberk writes to Bohuslav of Švamberk, her sister Lidmila's husband, asking that Katherine, a lady-in-waiting, be sent to her.*

21 December 1470, Třeboň
Czech Sedláček, *Sborník*

May this be given to the noble lord, Lord Bohuslav of Švamberk my lord and dear noble brother.

Noble lord and dear lord brother! I present my prayer to Your Grace. As I spoke with Your Grace in Zvíkov[93] about matters concerning Lady[94] Katherine, please know that today Zdebor of Kozí was sent to me by someone requesting that the maiden might come to me for the time of these festivals; and further, Conrad [of Petrovice][95] the burgrave will tell Your Grace why and for what reason. I ask Your Grace, if it seems [fitting] to Your Grace, please bring the maiden with you [so] that you might please send her to me for my comfort because I ask Your Grace [this favor]. Given in Třeboň on Friday before Jesus' birth 1470.

Anéžka of Rožmberk.

55. *Perchta of Rožmberk writes to her nephew[96] Henry of Rožmberk, who has taken over the government of the Rožmberk estates from his father John. Perchta has moved to Vienna and wants Henry to inform himself of her problems by consulting Jarohněv of Úsuší, a longtime Rožmberk servant and friend.*

31 January 1472, Vienna
German Třeboň, ms

Well-born lord and dear nephew, my friendly[97] service and good-will. I bring to your attention that I am writing to Jarohněv [asking him] to inform you about those issues related to my destitution, which he knows very well, and I ask you all, my dear kinsmen, that

---

[93] A Rožmberk castle where Švamberk was the governor.

[94] Anéžka addresses her as 'Lady' but refers to her as a maiden.

[95] Zdebor of Kozí and Conrad were both local petty noblemen loyal to the Rožmberks.

[96] The original, *vetter*, designated both the brother of one's father or the son of one's brother; in the plural it was used to designate male kin. Matthias Lexer, *Mittelhochdeutsches Taschenworterbuch* (34th edition, Leipzig: S. Hirzel Verlag, 1974), p. 287.

[97] The original, *freuntlich*, has the meaning of friendly, affectionately, and of kinship.

you will come and look at my miserable life and never withhold your counsel and aid from me, which I seek entirely from you and want always to earn affectionately, and thus may God keep you.

Given in Vienna on the Friday before Saint Dorothy's Day [6 February] 1472.

Perchta, born of Rožmberk, wife of John of Lichtenštejn of Mikulov.

56. *Perchta of Rožmberk writes to her nephew, Henry of Rožmberk, urging him to act. She stresses her friendship and kinship.*

10 November 1472, Vienna
German   Třeboň, ms

Well-born lord, dear nephew, first my friendly service always. I have actually emphasized rather strongly to the present bearer of this letter that he should bring my destitution before your kinship. I am moved to ask you affectionately to believe him this time as you would believe me myself, and thereby show yourself to me as affectionate and of good will, and [I hope] that you would not refuse me in this, since I have sought it [your help] as well as all friendship and goodness for myself wholly in you as my dear nephew. I want to become [a kinswoman] to you again altogether willingly and with friendship. Given in Vienna on Erich's[98] day [26 October] before Martin's 1472.

Perchta, born of Rožmberk and the wife of Lord John of Lichtenštejn.

57. *Perchta of Rožmberk writes her nephew Henry of Rožmberk, instructing him in what to ask her brother-in-law, Henry of Lichtenštejn, who is negligent in sending her dowry income. In a postscript she asks that her nephew send a dog to an Austrian nobleman she knows.*

6 May 1473, Vienna
German   Třeboň, ms

Well-born lord and dear nephew, my friendly service and good-will. I have written to your kinship in the very next [letter], of which

---

[98] *Erichtag.* Eric's day is on 26 October, but since she suggests the next day is St. Martin's, or 11 November, she may have meant St. Eugene's day, 10 November, as is suggested by a later hand in the margin of the original MS.

I have sent my kinsman [Reinprecht] of Walsee[99] a copy, and he will have the answer for you in Cáhlov[100] when you are together. No information has been brought to my attention from my kinsman, nor from you, as to how the matter has been settled. And, as yet, nothing has been arranged for me by Lord Henry of Lichtenštejn; he is to bring me 150 gulden [about 5,200 groschen] which had been arranged for me, and I am therefore in great need. I ask your kinship to speak amicably now with Lord Henry of Lichtenštejn, and to request on my account that the money be arranged and that henceforth it be transferred annually at the right time. And take the counsel of your servants and of other good people and relatives and friends as well. And I trust you, as my dear nephew, that you will allow yourself to be controlled by diligence in these matters as I have tried to do for my own benefit, and as a kinswoman, I always want to earn your [goodwill]. And I ask you to let me know through the Daiger ambassador,[101] if you are going to stay there for a while. If so, I will send my servant to you with a spoken message which should not be written. And does it seem to you that for me [the matter] is lost because of the words of Daiger against Lord Henry? Should it be that you do not want to receive my spoken message there, then let the above-mentioned words [Daiger's] against Lord Henry speak for themselves, and let me know whether you have your servant Jarohněv [of Úsuší][102] with you at this time. And I wish you much good and happiness in your affairs. Given in Vienna at Pentecost after the day of the finding of the Holy Cross [3 May] 1473.

Perchta, born of Rožmberk, wife of Lord John of Lichtenštejn of Mikulov.

Postscript

Dear nephew, I am sending you a letter from my lord of Mayburg in which he asks about a good dog. I especially ask you not to refuse him and to send him two which are still usable and to answer his letter promptly, letting him know what action you will take. Also, regarding what is thought about the Starchemberg[103] debt, dear nephew, do not refuse him against his will. Should you, however,

---

[99] Reinprecht married Perchta's aunt, Catherine, the sister of her father. *Listář a listinář*, 1, p. 1.

[100] Freistadt, a town in Upper Austria.

[101] Identity uncertain.

[102] A local member of the lesser nobility in Rožmberk service.

[103] Lord Rudiger Štorkenberger, a friend of Perchta's father.

not now want to pay him so soon, do send him a friendly letter; this [request] is to you as though I am standing for him.

58.   *Perchta of Rožmberk informs her nephew Henry of Rožmberk that her husband John has died. She asks him to send his servant, Martin Tulmacz, with her dowry letters in order to establish her rights to her property.*

21 August 1473, Vienna
German   Třeboň, ms

Well-born lord and dear nephew, my friendly service and goodwill. I am letting you know that my lord and husband has unfortunately been brought down by death, may God be merciful to him. At this time, I ask you that in this critical situation help be afforded me with respect to my last testament against that Lichtenštejn man [Henry]. I bring my claim before you as my dear nephew [and hope] for my own sake that you will not desert me, and I especially ask you about my last testament and my letter of confirmation, which is with you, that you will send them to me, into my hands, so that I can examine them exactly as they were when our lord sent them. And may it be ordered on my behalf that Martin Tulmacz, your servant, come to me; I believe you owe me this much as your kinswoman. I want to let you know that I now handle my affairs according to the counsel of my good lord and kinsman. It has always been a heartfelt joy to me to hear from you that you are doing well. Given in Vienna on Saturday before Saint Bartholomew's day [24 August] 1473.
Perchta, born of Rožmberk, widow of the blessed John of Lichtenštejn.

59.   *Perchta of Rožmberk enlists the help of Jarohněv of Úsuší, a longtime Rožmberk servant and friend and member of the local lesser nobility.*

27 August 1473, Vienna
German   Třeboň, ms

My service and good will, dear Jarohněv. I am writing to my dear nephew Lord Henry of Rožmberk, as you will hear from him by letter. I ask you with great urgency to see to it that no one but Martin Tulmacz is sent to me. And I look entirely to you, to take great care over this matter, and that through this messenger you will let him know for my sake whether I can be sure to expect him. Given in Vienna on 27 August 1473.

60. *Perchta of Rožmberk writes to her nephew, Henry of Rožmberk, repeating her request for the documents establishing her dowry. She informs him that she is also receiving counsel from Reinprecht of Wallsee, husband of her aunt Catherine of Rožmberk.*

1 October 1473, Vienna
German   Třeboň, ms

Well-born lord and dear nephew. My affectionate service and good will. I ask you affectionately, to send [direct] into my hands my letter of authority and my letter of confirmation related to it, with the counsel and assistance of my dear uncle Lord Reinprecht of Wallsee. When I write to him now, I will ask that he, with you, take care to see that the same letter[s] might arrive here safely, despite the dangers. I understand the situation to be that I will need the letters [because] I have not received a sincere final answer regarding my affairs from that Lichtenštejn man. But now my messenger is with him, and I anticipate that my affairs will be brought to a conclusion. And the way I am understood there will determine how I act in the future. I am always glad to hear from you, as my dear nephew, that you are doing well and are healthy, together with your family. And may I always be commended [to God], just as I fervently wish for you. Given in Vienna on Friday after Saint Michael's day [29 September] 1473.

61. *Perchta of Rožmberk writes again to a family friend, Jarohněv of Úsuší, asking for his help in getting her dowry papers and for information about her rights to other property she left behind when she and her daughter left her husband.*

1 October 1473, Vienna
German   Třeboň, ms

First, my willing service, dear Jarohněv. I ask you to be diligent in this matter about which I am now writing to my nephew, and about which you will soon find out. Would you kindly keep a copy of that letter in your hands, and, as I asked you earlier, let me know what rights according to Czech custom I have to the bridewain[104] which my husband of blessed [memory] left behind. And I tell you

---

[104] The original, *Varundenhab*. A bride's outfit or provisions, often in a chest filled with clothing, bedding, and household goods.

that when I, with my dear daughter of blessed [memory], rode away from my lord and husband of blessed [memory], he and his brother did not provide me with one good penny's worth. I add this to my letter so that you will be able to judge for yourself and know how to counsel me. Given in Vienna on Friday after Saint Michael's day [29 September] 1473.

Perchta, born of Rožmberk, widow of the blessed Lord John of Lichtenštejn.

62. *Perchta of Rožmberk informs her nephew, Henry of Rožmberk, that she will insist on her rights, and that he should act without delay on her behalf.*

7 January 1474, Vienna
German   Třeboň, ms

Well-born lord and dear nephew, my friendly service and good-will. I ask you not to rest from my affairs; do not accept any delay, and make it difficult for that [Henry of] Lichtenštejn to avoid the meeting in Linz; keep me informed straight away. I want to stand up for my [rights] with a legal transmitted letter of title; I declare on my own behalf that I will make use of it to the full extent of the law. No one will benefit if I allow the matter to stand any longer; with this be commended to God. Given in Vienna on Friday after the holy day of the three kings [6 January] 1474.

Perchta, born of Rožmberk, widow of the blessed Lord John of Lichtenštejn.

63. *Perchta of Rožmberk writes to Jarohněv of Úsuší a Rožmberk official, asking that he urge her nephew Henry to help her in her negotiations, saying she has no kin in Vienna to counsel her.*

20 January 1474, Vienna
German   Třeboň, ms

My service and goodwill, dear Jarohněv. I ask you to exert yourself with my dear nephew, so that there will be no rest, for you can well understand [the situation] from the answer of Lord Henry of Lichtenštejn and the friendly request which I have additionally made for myself; all of which he leaves out. And [he] puts forward to me that he wants to have a meeting with me here in the lower land [Lower Austria] in the presence of both our kin. He must be aware that I do not know of any blood kin I might have down here [Lower

Austria]. Also, I doubt everything he says and I could not honestly explain it to my kinsmen; [I do not know] on which day he wants to meet me, so I would not like to trouble you and other good people, for it might be in vain for my nephew to send them [in connection with] these matters. Given in Vienna on the day of St. Fabian and St. Sebastian [20 January] 1474.

Perchta, born of Rožmberk, widow of the blessed Lord John of Lichtenštejn.

64. *Perchta of Rožmberk to Přibik Hádkov of Paběnice, a local member of the gentry and official of Krumlov, urging that her nephew take action on the letter from Henry of Lichtenštejn.*

20 January 1474,Vienna
German   Třeboň, ms

My service and goodwill, dear Hettko [Přibik Hádkov]. I have received the notice, the answer of Lord Henry of Lichtenštejn, which you supplied to me through the efforts of my dear nephew of Rožmberk. Now I am writing to my dear nephew again, and I ask you to exert yourself on my behalf. As soon as he comes home, see that the letter is examined and read without delay. Given in Vienna on the day of St. Fabian and St. Sebastian [20 January].

Perchta, born of Rožmberk, widow of the blessed Lord John of Lichtenštejn.

65. *Perchta of Rožmberk writes to the Rožmberk official, Jarohněv of Úsuší, informing him that she is drafting a last will and that the lord of Wahrenberg, an acquaintance in Vienna, is pressing to have her nephew Henry pay an outstanding debt.*

29 June 1474, Vienna
German   Třeboň, ms[105]

To the noble Jarohněv of Úsuší my good friend. My friendly service and goodwill, dear Jarohněv. You wrote to me recently that you cannot come down to see me because you are so busy, and that my dear nephew, Lord Henry of Rožmberk, is willing to send you down

---

[105] The original does not appear to have survived. There are two copies in the Třeboň archive; one in a formal Gothic handwriting of the nineteenth century and one in the more free handwriting of a Rožmberk official, named Svetecký, from the eighteenth century. *AČ*, 11, p. 281. Where there are discrepancies I have followed the Svetecký version.

to me, [but you ask] whether there is such a great need: I ask you to kindly thank him fervently on my account, and I appeal to you to leave the great business in which you are involved and come down to me now because of my illness and suffering [which is] mostly why I have been longing for you to come. I have now partially settled the matter as best I could, and tell my dear nephew that I am not writing this with any pleasure. I have made a last will, in which I have not forgotten his [interests] as much as I was able, [and] as far as God has taken care of me. I would like you to [offer] aid and counsel so that the testament can be carried out; I have spoken with the [lord] of Wahrenberg about the 200 gulden [7,000 groschen]. I do not understand what he wants, but I know that he is greatly annoyed over this and he says that he well knows that my nephew could surely send the gulden securely if he wanted to. Therefore there is no point in me talking with him about this anymore, and it is not because of my nephew that I am causing him this delay. I always hope that all is well for you and that you are happy: hereby be commended to God. Given in Vienna on the day of the apostles St. Peter and St. Paul [29 June] 1474.

Perchta born of Rožmberk, now widow of the blessed John of Lichtenštejn.

66. *Gregory Klaryc writes to Conrad of Petrovice, the burgrave[106] in Český Krumlov, describing Anéžka's opposition to her nephew's use of her castle for his banquet, and describing a dispute between various members of the castle service staff and officials.*

28 August 1474, Třeboň
Czech   Sedláček, *Sborník*

Let this be given to my dear friend the noble squire Conrad of Petrovice, burgrave in Krumlov. First my service to the dear lord burgrave! Lord Jarohněv [of Úsuší] let me know that I should prepare a kitchen[107] for his Lord's Grace[108] at her Grace's, the maiden Anéžka; also that there should be wine, bread and other food at Her Grace's, so that the lords and the maidens [could] sit down together. And Maid Anéžka showed me the places which she has

---

[106] The governor of the castle.

[107] To be understood in the wider sense of meaning everything needed for preparing a banquet.

[108] One of her nephews.

filled up with her utensils, saying that other utensils and especially the kitchen cannot be [put there]. So I do not know where to locate [the banquet] other than on the ramparts; but Maid Catherine will be with Maid Anéžka and in order to get to the table, she will have to walk upon the wall.

Dear lord burgrave! I must complain about Rys to you; he took some puppy of a hunting dog in Zvíkov and said that Hodějovsky,[109] gave it to him because [the dog] bites hens to death, and the burgrave of Zvíkov[110] talks about me and slanders me and says that I stole the dog from him, while this is not the case, and so I am in disgrace because of Rys. And Rys knows how the burgrave helped him get the cross-bow which was stolen from him and he [the burgrave], because of this dog, has made other people angry with me. I ask and trust that you will speak to him about this and that you will order him to return the dog again. Given in Třebon on the Sunday after [the feast of] St. Bartholomew [24 August].
Gregory.

67. *Perchta of Rožmberk writes to Henry of Lichtenštejn, her brother-in-law, informing him that he is overdue in paying her dowry income.*

25 December 1474, Vienna
German   Třeboň, ms

Well-born lord and dear brother. My service and goodwill. As you must know, according to my authority and my letter, you and your brother now owe me 37,500 groschen[111] which you were to pay me on the preceding St. Gall's day (16 October). I ask you, as my dear brothers, to have the bailiff pay me instead of you and your brother, inasmuch as I will soon be in need of it. I also ask you to bring my affairs to an amicable conclusion with your brother, as you have just asked in your most recent letter to me and to my son; we fully trust you to do it soon, so that I will no longer be unpaid and overdue. And I have ordered my dear nephew to tell you something of what I would like. I absolutely request you, my dear brother, that you will give him [her nephew] in my stead an amicable [and] final

---

[109] A member of the lesser nobility, owner of Hodějov, loyal to the Rožmberks.
[110] Bohuslav of Švamberk, husband of Anéžka's sister Lidmila.
[111] The terms of her separation agreement are not known. Based on her dowry, she should have received at least 6,000 groschen a year, which means he had not delivered for at least six years.

answer; I believe you owe me this much. Given in Vienna on Sunday of the Christmas celebrations 1474.
P g v R H H v L S W.
[Her initials *Perkcht, geboren von Rosnbergk Hern Hannsen von Liechtenstain Seliger Witib*].
Perchta, born of Rožmberk, widow of the blessed Lord John of Lichtenštejn.

68. *Perchta of Rožmberk writes to her nephew, Henry of Rožmberk, that she is sending instructions through his servant, Martin Tulmacz.*

26 December 1474, Vienna
German   Třeboň, ms

Well-born lord and dear nephew, my friendly service and goodwill. I thank you sincerely for your friendly requests which you have recently made to me through your servant. Now I have ordered this Martin [Tulmacz] to let you know all about what I think [and] I ask you, all my dear kinsmen, that you will allow me to direct you in all this, and not rest from it. I believe you all owe me this much as my dear kinsmen. With this may you be commended unto the Lord God. Given in Vienna on St. Stephen's day during the Christmas celebrations 1474.
Perchta, born of Rožmberk, widow of the blessed Lord John of Lichtenštejn.

69. *Perchta of Rožmberk writes to her nephew, Henry of Rožmberk, that she thinks she has the plague.*[112]

25 October 1475, Vienna
German   Třeboň, ms

Well-born lord and dear nephew, first my friendly service, with goodwill. Because your servant has been with me, your servant Herman knows that I have had spots from the plague. Your servant will tell you all about this so that I can serve you, you should know that I am willing [to do so]. Also I heartily wish you to be happy and

---

[112] The original, *dass ich vlecz hab gehabt zu den pessten*. People in medieval and early-modern Europe gave the name plague or *pest* to any number of illnesses. Epidemics of the plague struck Europe on average every decade in the fifteenth century. Christopher Dyer, *Standards of Living in the Later Middle Ages* (Cambridge: Cambridge University Press, 1989), p. 271.

that everything is going well for you. Given on Wednesday after St. Luke's day [18 October].

Perchta, born of Rožmberk, widow of the blessed Lord John of Lichtenštejn.

70. *Anéžka of Rožmberk's last will and testament, describing the authority she enjoyed over the castle and estate of Třeboň, her interest in cattle, her membership of the family jointure and her charity towards her servants.*

2 October 1482, Třeboň
Czech   Sedláček, *Sborník*

My dear lords[113] and my dear cousins. According to the letter from You under Your seals and under the seal of Bohuslav of Švamberk[114] and of several other good people, as will be found in the aforementioned letter, in which letter at my request, with Your goodwill, it is approved by Your Graces that, whatever things I might have in the house, I am empowered to give, to dictate, to bequeath after my death, however and to whomever it will seem fitting to me. And I also have from Your Graces a second [letter] with your seals attached, stating that the several calves and cattle, which I carefully tended for my living, and which I have among the people, I can dispose of and give where it seems fit to me, as the aforementioned letter further indicates to Your Graces: let all that is in the court and what belongs to it insofar as the dear God allowed me to hold it, be given to Your Graces after my death, but I ask that you might please remember, as I requested a letter from Your Graces to this effect, that whoever survives me in my court shall be allowed to remain here after my death for one year, so that in that year he can prepare other lodging for himself; please do not ask them to move out against their will within a year.

I leave a written note for Your Graces of what was rendered to me each year, let it be rendered to Your Graces this year too, and also I leave a list of what is owing so that it remains as part of the court. And whatever else there is besides what is written down, it belongs to that one [of her four nephews] who will reside after me in the [Třeboň] court: I ask that with these [words], he be released. As it stands written in the main letter, you are required to give 6,000 groschen within a year wherever and to whomever I might bequeath

---

[113] Her nephews, Henry, Vok, Peter, and Ulrich.
[114] Husband of Anéžka's sister Lidmila.

it. I trust Your Graces, as my dear cousins, that you will be pleased to graciously bring this about, that you will graciously look after and effect this, remembering my faith towards you, which I have had up to my last hours; that I have not required anything difficult of you concerning this estate and this kinship, in which I remained united with your father, and therefore with you also, being the heir of this estate; just as your father and you also, never disassociated yourselves [from the inheritance], so have I not.[115] And whoever might show this letter to Your Graces and who might have the main letter in his power, I ask that the testament might also remain in effect for him or for this person as I give it to him through this letter and make him the executor in authority of everything that is mentioned above. For my better security in this, I ordered my seal to be attached to this letter and I requested the noble squire John of Trnová, at this time the captain[116] in Třeboň, that he order his seal to be attached next to mine as further witness; however without any prejudice to himself or his heirs. Given in Třeboň the fourth day after the feast of Saint Wenceslas [28 September] in 1482.

---

[115] Anéžka stresses that she has not taken advantage of Czech custom, according to which, when members of the family had received their shares of the patrimony, they were declared as disassociated from the family for property purposes only and had no further claim to the inheritance.

[116] Responsible for the military aspects and defence of the castle.

Interpretive Essay

Self and Family in the Letters of Perchta of Rožmberk

The letters of the Rožmberk sisters are above all important for the light they shed on the lives of two self-assured noblewomen. The more abundant letters of Perchta illustrate sharply how she coped with unhappiness within a social and cultural context which required females to devalue themselves and submit their wills to those of males. At first glance Perchta appears ineffective and her letters reveal a society and a culture in which women basically have no power whatsoever. Power can, however, be seen as something that comes and goes in a person's life, and as something even the weakest of people possess.[1] Perchta's letters show that she had the ability to mobilize people around her and to persuade them to act on her behalf and thus change the circumstances of her life. Her power was based on a strategy in which she carefully observed the limits that her status as a wife placed on her. At the same time she knew herself as a person born into a proud aristocratic family, and this gave her confidence to claim her rights as a human being. Important to the success of her strategy was her close bond with her father and brothers to whom she addressed her letters, as well as her relationship to her more distant kin and her servants.

Perchta, like other medieval women, experienced the dissonance of being a medieval woman. She had to accept a definition of herself as inferior by birth. Medieval women who wanted to be effective accepted a lesser status as part of their strategy to influence events. They consented to a social position defined as inferior, but proceeded to act as persons who shared or participated in a common humanity with males. The social, political, and cultural arbiters of the time defined women as not capable of being educated, unable to interpret theological texts, unworthy to lead in the church's liturgical exercises, and not competent to conduct war and govern

---

[1] See Pauline Stafford, 'Emma: The Powers of the Queen in the Eleventh Century', in *Queens and Queenship in Medieval Europe*, ed. Anne Duggan (Woodbridge: Boydell Press, 1997), p. 1, and Vaclav Havel, *The Power of the Powerless* (Armonk NY: M. E. Sharpe, 1985), *passim*.

society. As Luce Irigaray expresses it, there was only one sex that spoke, one sex that made the laws.[2] But medieval women also had a sense of self-respect, whether learned or innate. As a result they struggled with a certain discord in understanding their status. They felt that the cultural values that represented men as privileged to act and to initiate, and women to be passive and to accept, did not accurately reflect what they believed about themselves. For this reason women accepted or mimicked their male-defined lesser status because it gave them an opportunity to participate in cultural and political life. Once they acknowledged their inferiority women were less of a threat to men and they could proceed to express their own feelings, ideas, values, and aspirations. Women wore the cloak of passivity and submission while speaking with the voice of conviction and insistence.

Medieval women such as Perchta showed a willingness to accept a lower social status as women, but presented another face in which they revealed their sense of personhood. Such women could not hide their fundamental notion of their own dignity and capacity. There are a number of examples of medieval women subverting a submissive social status by living a dynamic life. Radegund, the sixth-century princess whose land was devastated by the Franks, wore the mask of weakness and suffering while at the same time assertively achieving goals and enforcing her will.[3] Hildegard of Bingen, the twelfth-century German nun famous for her enormous activity in areas forbidden to women such as preaching and writing, also presented herself as a fragile human being, 'made of ashes and of filth, timid, simple and untaught'.[4] Her adoption of lowly status was strategically effective because she made it work for her by deciding when to write and when not to, when to refuse God's command and

---

[2] Luce Irigaray, *This Sex Which is not One,* trans. Catherine Porter (Ithaca: Cornell University Press, 1985), p. 30. Irigaray argues that there exists a feminine voice which needs to be prized out of the components of the masculine philosophical discourse (p. 74).

[3] Karen Cherewatuk, 'Radegund and Epistolary Tradition', in *Dear Sister: Medieval Women and the Epistolary Tradition,* ed. Karen Cherewatuk and Ulrike Wiethaus (Philadelphia: University of Pennsylvania Press, 1993), pp. 20–39.

[4] Samuel Lyndon Gladden, 'Hildegard's Awakening: A Self-Portrait of Disruptive Excess', in *Representations of the Feminine in the Middle Ages,* ed. Bonnie Wheeler (Cambridge: Academia Press, 1993), pp. 224–32. Compare also Paula Martin, 'A Brightness of Purple Lightening: Hildegard of Bingen's Self-Perception', in the same volume, pp. 244–45, and Gillian T. W. Ahlgren, 'Visions and Rhetorical Strategy in the Letters of Hildegard of Bingen', in Cherewatuk and Wiethaus, pp. 49–52.

when to obey. Similarly, Maria de Hout (d. 1547) accepted herself as an abject sinner bent on self-destruction when writing to her confessor, but in a close circle of female friends she appeared confident and triumphant describing her spiritual achievements frankly and unselfconsciously.[5]

The fifteenth-century Italian-French writer Christine of Pizan was exceptional when she openly stated that the social construction of woman as weak and unlearned was inherently destructive of women's humanity. According to Christine, women did not lose their femininity and become masculine by intellectual learning, nor was there anything eternally and essentially feminine about ignorance and inferiority.[6] Christine made explicit what women such as Perchta felt and lived – their conviction of female ontological participation in humanity.

While it is true that many medieval women, including Perchta of Rožmberk, represented themselves as deserted and mistreated, reduced to lamenting and begging for help, there are limits to the usefulness of the 'suffering woman' motif. Christine de Pizan explained the prevalent tone of suffering in the writings of women not as an essentially feminine characteristic but as the result of the double standard between the sexes.[7] Lamentation and desperation are the theme of many of the letters written by late fifteenth-century aristocratic women in the Holy Roman Empire, such as Amilie of Pfalz-Zweibrücken-Veldenz. Amilie frequently complained about miserable living conditions, alienation, and loneliness, and wrote to father or brother for comfort, refuge, and help. Cordula Nolte finds the letters of German aristocratic women somewhat formulaic, but rightly declines to see them as a topos because the individual women describe their differing experiences.[8] Before we treat women's

---

[5]   Ulrike Wiethaus, ' "If I had an Iron Body": Maria de Hout', in Cherewatuk and Wiethaus, pp. 183–89.

[6]   Earl Richards, ' "Seulette a part" – The "Little Woman on the Sidelines" Takes up her Pen: The Letters of Christine de Pizan', in Cherewatuk and Wiethaus, pp. 139–60.

[7]   Richards, 'Seulette a part', p. 142.

[8]   See Cordula Nolte, '*Pey eytler finster in einem weichen pet geschrieben.* Eigenhänduge Briefe in der Familienkorrespondenz der Markgrafen von Brandenburg (1470–1530)', in *Adelige Welt und familiäre Beziehung*, ed. Heinz-Dieter Heimann, pp. 177–202, and her unpublished paper, 'Überlegungen zu eigenhändigen Familienbriefen: Die Korrespondenz Amilies von Pfalz-Zweibrücken-Veldenz mit ihren Eltern, Kurfurst Albrecht Achilles und Anna von Brandenburg', delivered at the Conference *Die private Welt des Adels in Selbstzeugnissen*, Potsdam, 22–25 October, 1997. I wish to thank the author for providing me with a copy of her paper.

writing as a type or genre, it is important to take note of women of achievement such as Barbara of Brandenburg, who in 1433 as a ten-year-old was married to the son of the duke of Mantua. She accepted life in a new family and country, learned a foreign language and played an active role in the family into which she married, and wrote letters reflecting her accomplishments.[9] In other words, women wrote about their joys and accomplishments as well as about their grief and suffering, just as men did.[10]

We cannot establish women's writing as a genre, whether it is about affliction or anything else, simply because the writers have female bodies, as Albrecht Classen does in his 1988 article, 'Female Epistolary Literature from Antiquity to the Present: An Introduction'.[11] Although Classen effectively made the case that what women have written in letters is an important contribution to culture, his attempt to establish a female epistolary genre is contradicted by his own material. He showed that medieval and Reformation women, just like men, wrote about public, religious, and theological issues, that Italian renaissance women 'paralleled the male counterparts in all respects',[12] and that sixteenth-century French women letter-writers were not characterized by passion, what Classen refers to as the hallmark of women's writing. It is preferable not to think of female letter-writing as a specific literary category because we cannot define an epistolary genre as a cultural model when it is based on the physical form and composition of the writer rather than on the style or content of the letter. The category 'women' is variable and incomplete and for this reason it must remain a permanently available site of contested meanings.[13] Letters and other writing which reflects private and intimate dialogue,

---

[9]   Katherine Walsh, 'Verkaufte Töchter? Überlegungen zu Aufgabenstellung und Selbstvertgefühl von in die Ferne verheirateten Frauen anhand ihrer Korrespondenz', *Jahrbuch des Vorarlberger Landesmuseumsvereins* 135 (1991), pp. 129–44.

[10] On the affliction topos, see Cherewatuk and Wiethaus, p. 14. See also Philip Braunstein, 'The Emergence of the Individual: Toward Intimacy. The Fourteenth and Fifteenth Centuries', in *Revelations of the Medieval World*, eds Georges Duby and Philippe Ariès, vol. 2, *A History of Private Life* (Cambridge MA: Harvard University Press, 1988), p. 540, for non-gendered writing about suffering.

[11] In *Studia Neophilologica* 60 (1988), pp. 2, 5, and 7.

[12] Classen, 'Female Epistolary', p. 6.

[13] Judith Butler, *Gender Trouble: Feminism and the Subversion of Identity* (New York: Routledge, 1990), pp. 2–3, 6, 15. See Rosi Braidotti, 'Comment on Felski's "The Doxa of Difference": Working through Sexual Difference', *Signs: Journal of Women in Culture and Society* 23 (1997), p. 35.

whether written by men or women, are important because they give us an entrance into the writer's self-understanding. The correspondence of Perchta and Anéžka of Rožmberk with their family and friends allows us in the same way to recognize the emergence of a self-understanding which struggled against the identity that social and cultural norms of the day had formed in women.

When writers described their pain and sorrow they may well have done so to sway their readers as part of a rhetorical strategy influenced by epistolary and literary traditions. As a result, letters may only partially mirror the facts of the writer's life. The eyes of those who write about their own lives, looking inward, see no more innocently than do the eyes of those who write about events of the outside world.[14] Still, human suffering is real and medieval women wrote about it. It is not necessary, even if it were possible, to rate or evaluate objectively the level of a medieval person's misery. What we can do is examine and describe the circumstances of individuals whose lives we find recorded, and understand how they dealt with their situation.

Perchta of Rožmberk's power was her ability to persuade others and to mobilize them into action on her behalf. Her letters reveal that she followed a strategy which recognized her domestic status as an obedient wife, subordinate to the men of her family. They also show that her acceptance of a dependent female status had limits. She superimposed her identity as a person with rights to dignity and respect upon her passive quiescent self as a wife. Her letters express her belief in herself as a person who deserved better than she got in marriage. She had the self-confidence to think that her personal needs were important enough to warrant burdening other people with them, and to construct her argument so persuasively that her readers were compelled to respond to her complaints.

Despite dashed hopes of her family and husband, Perchta retained her dignity throughout her married life, which we can divide into four stages. The first stage (1449–52) was her discovery of her lonely and powerless position as a new bride whose dowry had not been delivered and with an indifferent if not hostile husband. The second stage (1453–63) began with the arrival of dowry installments and then its full delivery in 1460. Perchta had a few happy years, as her letters to her father and her brother John show (Letters 27 and 34). She and her husband ate together and shared each other's

---

[14] Braunstein, 'The Emergence', p. 535.

company on other occasions. By 1461 the disputes over property among her in-laws again began to disturb her peace as her husband's kin threatened her right to the estate on which her dowry was guaranteed. In late 1463 she decided that the living conditions with her husband and his family were intolerable and she made arrangements to leave him. Taking her daughter with her, she moved home to Český Krumlov. Her last letters from her husband's home were in December 1463 (Letters 39 and 40). Her kin were still negotiating with her husband in 1465 (Letters 42, 43, 47, and 48) and sometime during that year Perchta left her husband. The third stage (1465–72), was spent in Český Krumlov, the castle of her childhood. She seems to have been content (or communicated orally) and it is not until February 1470 that she wrote her brother that her husband's income payments to her were in arrears (Letters 50–52). The last stage of her life began in early 1472, after her nephew Henry took over the lordship of Český Krumlov from his father, her brother John (Letters 55–65 and 67–69). Because she was not as close to her nephew as she had been to John, at the age of forty-one, she left her childhood home. She did not join her sister in Třeboň, but moved to Vienna, most likely into the Benedictine monastery of the Scots, where she was eventually interred.[15] Most of her letters from Vienna are concerned with collecting her incomes. In her last letter, in October 1475, she writes that she thinks she has the plague because she has discovered spots on her face (Letter 69). She died the next year.

Perchta's early training as a young girl prepared her to submit her own wishes in order to serve her family's interest by marrying the man whom her father chose. She understood the expectation that as a wife she had to obey. The training she received was drawn from moralists and preachers whose ideas were similar to those of Thomas of Štítný.[16] Perchta had learned that men ruled the home and that she was expected to submit herself to them. At the same time her upbringing had prepared her to anticipate companionship as well as authority and respect in her married household. It is evident from Perchta's words (Letters 34 and 39) that she expects to be with her husband; to converse, dine, and sleep with him.

---

[15] Anna Skýbová, *Listy Bílé Paní Rožmberské* [The Letters of the White Lady of Rožmberk] (Prague: Panorama, 1985), p. 27. Duke Henry II in 1155 invited Irish-Scottish monks from Regensburg to a house in Vienna. In 1418 it became a German-speaking house.

[16] See above, Introduction, p. 9.

Perchta's disappointment was that Lichtenštejn had no interest in her company (Letters 13 and 15). Failing friendship from her husband, Perchta knew that she should still expect to be next to him on the ladder of the domestic hierarchy, running the household and having the money necessary for hiring staff and purchasing supplies.[17] Perchta accepted the need for wifely obedience but she also expected mutual respect and wifely authority.

Perchta also understood her need to obey her father and brothers, even though the salutations or introductions in her letters to them are remarkably free of the 'rhetoric of service' common in the letters of German, English, and French aristocratic children. Medieval protocol allowed for a variety of ways to begin one's letters, but generally the greater the social divide between writer and addressee, the more excessive the writer's claim to condescension.[18] The discourse of obedience was well-known in the Rožmberk household. Perchta's brother John, for example, in letters to his father, described himself as an obedient son even after his father had designated him joint administrator of the estates. In her salutations Perchta did not rely on formal phrases of deference to win over her readers but adapted etiquette to her own state of mind. Her greetings were almost always free of submission and consisted of sending her prayers and wishing the recipient good health. For example, her letter in 1451 to her brother Henry begins 'To my dear brother, the noble lord, Lord Henry of Rožmberk. I send you my prayers, my noble lord and dear brother! It would make me happy to know that you are well' (Letter 17). Perchta generally addressed her father and brothers as 'Your Grace' and referred to her husband as her lord, but rarely did her letters begin with a promise of obedience or service.

Insofar as her introductions are any indication, Perchta saw herself as an equal member of her family. She began her letters in a forthright if not curt fashion. This is apparent in the letter of 20 February 1450, when for the first time she brought her complaint against her father and informed him of her unhappiness. After the obligatory naming of the addressee, she dispensed with a greeting

---

[17] Emilie Amt, ed., *Women's Lives in Medieval Europe* (London: Routledge 1993), pp. 323–30.

[18] Diane Watt, ' "No Writing for Writing's Sake": The Language of Service and Household Rhetoric in the Letters of the Paston Women', in Cherewatuk and Wiethaus, p. 127. See also Catherine Moriarty, ed., *The Voice of the Middle Ages in Personal Letters: 1100–1500* (New York: Peter Bedrick Books, 1989). For the standard medieval epistolary form, see Cherewatuk and Wiethaus, pp. 4–5. For German letters see, Nolte, *'Pey etlicher fenster'*, pp. 177–202.

and launched into the purpose and argument of her letter. The letter begins 'Let this be given to my dear lord, my father, Lord Ulrich of Rožmberk. And dear lord! That which I wrote you in my first letter, that I am doing well, is unfortunately not so; would that I was doing well' (Letter 7). In July 1451, she begins a letter to her brother Henry with the briefest of salutations: 'Dear brother, As I wrote that my lord [Lichtenštejn] was still in Vienna, therefore you should know, dear brother, that he came home on Tuesday, on St. Margaret's Day' (Letter 19; see also Letters 14 and 15). Perchta wrote from her heart as if to say, 'I am who I am. Take my message for what it is.' She dictated her letters in direct speech, as she had conversed in the household of her childhood. In her urgent appeals to her father and brother to address themselves to her misery, she counted on her own words and language and rejected recourse to the flattery which was present in the formulas of service.

Perchta included the offer of service in the introductions to her letters only after her problem seemed to be resolved and when writing to her nephew. Her letter to her father in 1454 is instructive (Letter 27). She informs him that she and her husband had become reconciled and had pledged to live together honorably, faithfully and lovingly. She asks for nothing from her father except that he rejoice with her. The letter was written by a German secretary, probably in her husband's employ, and it began with the words, 'I offer my willing and obedient service'. This was also the formula for her letters to her nephew, Henry (Letters 55, 56, and others), also written in German. She had not grown up with Henry in the same household and the distance she felt from him is evident. Her address of service may also reflect her German-speaking secretary's preference. While Perchta's forms of address avoided excessive deference, in the message of her letters, she was careful to present herself as meek and docile.

As part of her letter-writing strategy, Perchta scrupulously adhered to the spirit if not the rhetoric of a daughter's and wife's need to obey. In her first two letters to her father from her new home she remained silent about her troubles. She brought no complaint against her father or her husband and wrote that she was doing well, although she longed for her father (Letters 5 and 6). Some three months after her wedding she told a different story. She revealed that she had concealed the true state of her marriage because she wanted to fulfill her assigned role of submission and her place in her father's marriage strategy. On 20 February 1450 she writes 'That which I wrote you in my first letter, that I am doing well, that unfortunately is not so, ... on the contrary I am doing very badly' (Letter 7). Despite her disclosure that her father had served her poorly in choosing her husband, she maintains her stance of a deferential and submissive daughter. She characterizes her letter as 'my humble request', and assures her father that she has written to others that she is doing well. She knew she was asking her father to do something improper when she asked him to send one of his men to look into the domestic sphere of another noble lord. Her father's request that she not speak about this matter to anyone else reflected well the uncomfortable position in which her letter placed him.

Perchta also pointed out that she had not crossed the line of what was proper behavior for a wife. In 1450 her brother Henry joined her father in telling her to keep silent and not to cause trouble and embarrassment. She responds that she will be happy to comply, saying: 'Dear lord, I will gladly do it', but she also takes great pains to point out bluntly that she has complied with the accepted social norms requiring wifely obedience (Letter 10). Her decision to write and complain had not come from her own initiative but from friendly noblemen who had seen the circumstances of her life. Perchta writes that one of these noblemen, Lord Aleš of Šternberk, had learned about her life from others, not from her. In her words,

> he [Šternberk] said many things to me, about what my conditions were, which he had learned from others, not from me; also, he was with us for a good while, and I cannot deny all this what he saw with his own eyes. And when I could not deny it, only then did I agree that he could let the lord [Rožmberk] know. (Letter 10).

A daughter and a sister did not place her kin in the difficult position of confronting her husband. Ill will between two families whose children had been given in marriage meant that the father's marriage plan had been a miscalculation, if not a complete failure. To admit negotiating a mismatch was serious enough for a father, but to take action to alleviate a daughter's unhappiness required even greater embarrassment and interference in the lordship of a fellow-nobleman. Perchta knew that by presenting her father with her complaint she placed his anticipated gains from the marriage in jeopardy, so to clear herself of possible blame she writes to her father on 31 December 1450 saying, 'God knows that I am without fault in what is happening to me, that in me he has a faithful wife' (Letter 16). On 13 July 1451 she makes the same point to her brother Henry: 'Although it is I who am writing about myself, that I am not guilty towards him [her husband] in any way, I trust God that you will not see it otherwise' (Letter 17). Even while protesting and acting to improve her life, Perchta retained her position as the obedient wife: she had fulfilled the requirements that society and culture asked of her.

Perchta attempted to remain loyal to her husband even when the companionship she sought in marriage did not materialize. In 1454 her family began supplying her dowry in regular installments. For a brief period her husband was friendly to her and it seems that the couple pledged anew to uphold their wedding vows. On 29 July 1454 she writes that her husband had undertaken to be devoted and kind to her and that she would do as she had promised and continue to be a loving wife (Letter 27). In December 1463, fourteen years after her wedding, she described another brief respite from her unhappiness (Letter 39). She expressed her pleasure with her husband's willingness to eat with her and keep her company. But this bliss soon ended. Although she offered him her energy and her material resources to resolve a sticky financial transaction, as soon as he had her money he turned away from her again. In summing up her disappointment she repeats her loyalty and the support which she had offered as a wife: 'I am afraid that in the end no [lasting] good will come of all this, but I do not regret, nor do I want to regret, that I showed him faithfulness, the lord God will be my reward' (Letter 39 Postscript). Her concluding words paraphrase those of the preacher Thomas of Štítný, who counseled unhappy wives to remain loving towards their husbands in anticipation of a heavenly recompense. Her correspondence shows, though, that she was not willing to wait until she reached heaven to attain God's comfort. All her life she acted to gain security, comfort, and happiness here on earth.

Perchta's awareness of herself as a mistreated human being was born when she saw herself in perspective: when she saw that her socially defined status as a wife was not how she envisioned her life as a person. As Philip Braunstein observes, when people sense themselves set apart from others the results can lead to a radical questioning of the social order.[19] Perchta's doubts about wifely submission led her eventually to leave her husband and lord and return to her childhood home. She needed to harmonize her self-perception as a person who had a right to happiness with the inferior identity of an amenable uncomplaining wife ascribed to her by the forces of power in her society. She could not accept the reality of her

---

[19] Braunstein, 'The Emergence of the Individual', p. 536.

marriage, which fell short of what she expected. As a wife she was not supposed to challenge her husband and lord, but as a human being she could not tolerate her situation. Consequently she adjusted her ideas on wifely duties, and it was a wife's obligation to submit that she subordinated to her right as a woman to happiness.

Her sense of self began with her identity in a specific family. Her expectations were those of a woman born and raised a Rožmberk. Her signature in her Czech letters was simply 'Perchta of Rožmberk', reflecting the importance she placed on her family of birth. In her German letters she was 'Perchta born of Rožmberk, the wife of Lord John of Lichtenštejn and of Mikulov', or a variation thereof.[20] Perchta did not see herself as an inactive object of exchange between families in which she had to accept one patronym for another. By retaining her name of birth she made clear that she had not been absorbed into her husband's family but was holding on to her own. Her father sought to lessen her identification with the name of her family of birth because he recognized that her courage to resist was boosted by it. In his letter to Perchta in November 1450, he tries to encourage her to identify with her husband by leaving out any reference to her Rožmberk name and addressing her as 'Noble lady, Lady Perchta of Lichtenštejn and of Mikulov' (Letter 12). Her father presumably hoped that if his daughter thought of herself as a Lichtenštejn she would cease troubling him with her difficulties. In her case the social bond between two families, between the men who had established the marriage, broke down. The Rožmberk–Lichtenštejn alliance had collapsed when and because Perchta decided she was not prepared to tolerate her living conditions.

The wellspring of Perchta's self-confidence was her family home, where her warm relations with father and siblings had established her sense of worth. Both hers, and her sister's, words to their father and brothers, and theirs to them, reflect close ties of affection. Anéžka calls her youngest brother 'My dear little Johnny' (Letter 49) and Perchta expresses concern for John's wife and children

---

[20] 'Perchta geporen von Rosenberg Herren Hannsen von Lichtenstein von Nicolsperg gemähel.' SOA, *Cizí*, nos. 546, 582, 583, *passim*. The German letters may have been more subject to epistolary formula than the Czech ones in which she most likely collaborated only with her own secretary. See František Dvorský, *Perchta z Rožmberka zvaná bílá pání* [Perchta of Rožmberk, called the White Lady] (Prague, 1874, Matice lidu ročníku VIII. Čislo 2), p. 79. See also Georges Duby, *The Knight, the Lady, and the Priest: The Making of Modern Marriage in Medieval France* (Chicago: University of Chicago Press, 1993), p. 45.

(Letter 52). John in turn compares Perchta to a lover (Letter 41). Interactions and discussions with her brothers and with prominent guests[21] helped her to think of herself as a person with value. As a married woman she later reminded her brother that she was acting just as he had asked her to (Letter 10). She was careful, however, to observe the lay preacher Thomas of Štitný's caution not to cast a shadow on her husband's status by enhancing that of her own family. If she should represent herself as too haughty, she would undermine her strategy of getting her kin to act on her behalf. The insistent tone of her letters, her readiness to act and her chosen signature, 'Perchta of Rožmberk', show that she shared her family's sense of status, reflected in her brother Henry's request to John of Lichtenštejn that he treat his sister lovingly because she deserves it as a Rožmberk and as Lichtenštejn's wife.[22] From her awareness of being a Rožmberk, Perchta's self-perception moved to her sense of dignity as a person with basic rights.

Her letter to her father on 20 February 1450 (Letter 7), three months after her wedding, repudiates her earlier message of contentment and explains that she is distressed because her expectation of having authority in the household had not materialized. She had to defer in everything to her mother-in-law, who retained the position of the household manager and who disliked her. As the wife, by rights the second in authority, Perchta had no access to money with which to organize the Lichtenštejn household economy, nor to provide for her own needs. Perchta presents her letter as a formal complaint such as one might bring before a court of law:

> the complaint I bring before Your Grace is that I am in such a disorderly residence that there is no way I can get used to it. I am a veritable beggar of that lady and have to wait for everything from her hands. (Letter 7)

Perchta knew that in addition to what she could get on the strength of her relationship to her father, she also had a moral claim. So in December of the same year she appeals to divine authority, stating her belief that her father would someday encounter God as a judge in her suit against him. 'For you should know, she writes, that I have become so desperate that if you do not save me from this [situation], I shall bring a complaint against you before the Lord God' (Letter 16, Postscript).

---

[21] Skýbová, *Listy*, p. 23.
[22] This letter is available only in summary form in *AČ*, 11, ed. p. 251.

Despite the tears, the loneliness, and the despair that characterize many of her epistles, her entire correspondence reflects a campaign conducted with self-confidence by a woman aware of her innate status as a human being. In her letter to her father on 22 November 1450, Perchta makes explicit her claims based on birth, in other words, her rights as a person. She writes:

> It would be better that the day that saw me born had rather seen me dead, ... Therefore, dear lord, dear father, have compassion on me, as a father towards his children, and bear in mind, dear lord, that it was not my wish to be married. And I have called for and pleaded for help, which is my right as a child of its father; and remember, dear lord, your own blood-kin, for the sake of God's mercy. (Letter 13)

Perchta reiterates her human status in late December 1450 (Letter 16). Writing to her father, she reminds him that she is his child and that he should have buried her rather than married her to Lichtenštejn, and pointing out that there is a limit to the shame a person can humanly bear. Her words are rich with meaning. She had decided that her obligations as a daughter and a wife had to take second place to her status as a human being. Her appeal to kindred ties and to memories of childhood and fatherly care indicate that she remembered her family home as a congenial place, and the people with whom she had shared living space while growing up were her friends. Her references to her birth also draw attention to her status as a human being. Implicit in her words is the idea that males and females share the reality of beginning life in the same way. The life-giving event called birth does not distinguish between girls and boys. Sisters and brothers are the progeny of the same two people, and from that perspective birth provides the terms of discourse for a collective existence or ontology for both sexes.

Perchta had a visceral belief that she had rights by birth no matter how the law may have defined her. The late fifteenth-century Czech jurist, Kornel of Všehrd, explaining the social position of a wife, described her as legally unfree and as a captive, forced to do what her husband wants her to.[23] It is doubtful whether she had knowledge of a systematic legal and philosophical explanation of the rights of captives as laid out by the famous master of the University

---

[23] *M. Viktorina ze Všehrd O právích země české* [Master Viktorine of Všehrd, About the Laws of the Czech Land], ed. Hermenegild Jireček (Prague: Všehrd, 1874), pp. 228–29.

of Paris Henry of Ghent in 1289. Henry explained that even a prisoner had not only the right but the duty to preserve his life. His argument was picked up by Jacques Almain in 1500, who wrote that even a prisoner, 'by natural law is bound to preserve the life of his body'.[24] Perchta did not need the legal and philosophical explanation to understand her own right to preserve her life which to her father she represented as the rights of a child owed to her by her father.

In thinking of herself as a person with inherent dignity and status, Perchta was part of late medieval thought on the self. Since the twelfth century, European thinkers had examined the nature of the self and the boundary between oneself and the other. The discovery of the inner person involved the belief that human beings were made in the image of God. Increasingly, the men and women of the late Middle Ages defined the meaning of their lives by actively participating in the Christian religion.[25] They assumed that the divine image meant the same for all human beings, both male and female. Such thinking was at the heart of a subjectivized piety centered on the existential needs of the individual, and it fostered new forms of self-consciousness and personal identity. In Bohemia, such popular religious movements culminated in the Hussite reform and revolution. John Hus encouraged both men and women to take responsibility for their own salvation and to contribute to the Church's revitalization. Perchta's grandmother and her father in his youth were sympathetic to Hus's reform movement. Perchta herself showed no sympathy for the changes sought by the Hussite revolution, but she appropriated a widespread cultural spirit of choosing for oneself since self-definition was not limited to the religious sphere.

Perchta's view of herself accorded with notions of the self prevailing in late medieval Europe. She saw herself in terms used by philosophers such as Abélard, Thomas Aquinas, and others, even

---

[24] Brian Tierney, *The Rights of Natural Law: Studies on Natural Rights, Natural Law and Church Law 1150–1625*, no. 5 of Emory University Studies in Law and Religion (Atlanta GA: Scholars Press, 1997), pp. 83–88.

[25] Carolyn W. Bynum, *Jesus as Mother: Studies in the Spirituality of the High Middle Ages* (Berkeley: University of California Press, 1982), pp. 82, 87–89; Howard Kaminsky, 'The Problematics of Later Medieval Heresy', in *Husitství, Reformace, Renesance*, ed. Jaroslav Pánek et al. (Prague: Historical Institute, 1994), vol. 1, p. 151; and Herbert Grundmann, *Religiöse Bewegungen im Mittelalter* (Hildesheim: G. Olm, 1970), *passim*. See Introduction above, p. 3, for the Hussites.

though most probably she had no direct access to their works. Like Aquinas, she knew she would not find herself only by casting off an inhibiting pattern of thought – in her case wifely submission – but by adopting an appropriate affirmative one – her consciousness as a human being. Like Aquinas she saw that a human was someone with the capacity to provide for oneself and for others and as possessing knowledge of what was good and what evil. She could also affirm the general view as expressed by Marsiglio of Padua (1280–1343) that humans by nature desire a sufficient and satisfactory life.[26] Perchta's appeal to her father was based on birth. Her noble ancestry made it easier to claim birth rights, but implied in this demand was the notion of equality with her brother, even if she could not express gender parity given the social and cultural framework of late medieval Europe. Perchta rooted her self-perception in the fact of common or shared birth which provided the terms of discourse to argue for the rights for all men, present in the 1381 Peasants' Revolt in England, the fifteenth-century radical Hussites, and the sixteenth-century German peasants, and eventually extending to women in the French revolution.[27]

Perchta's letters to her father in February and November 1450 (Letters 7, 9 and 13) signaled that she was no longer a silent submissive wife, but one who was speaking out. She indicated that subjecting her needs and wants to her passive identity no longer served her purposes. The remnants, or perhaps the wreckage, of wifely subordination remained, but hers was henceforth a vocal and active compliance. In other words, her identity as a quiescent wife coexisted with that of a person confident and sure of herself and able to articulate her desires. She assumed the prevailing female role deliberately, and converted this form of subordination into an affirmation of herself. Perchta was not the first nor the last woman or man to take on more than one identity and to function well in the belief that all of them are true and genuine.[28]

---

[26] Anthony Black, *Political Thought in Europe 1250–1450* (Cambridge: Cambridge University Press, 1992), pp. 38, 63.

[27] See particularly the statement of the German peasants 'Although by rights every man is born free', in *Manifestations of Discontent in Germany on the Eve of the Reformation*, ed. Gerhard Strauss (Bloomington: University of Indiana Press, 1971), p. 165. This is not to suggest a genealogical connection between Perchta's appeal to her rights by birth and the Enlightenment's discussion of the rights of man and woman.

[28] See Ulrike Wiethaus, 'If I had an Iron Body', p. 188, and Judith Butler, *Bodies that Matter* (New York: Routledge, 1993), especially pp. 3–7.

Perchta believed that the essence of being human was a certain quality of moral behavior towards others. The way one person treated another determined one's status. Human beings had feelings and sensitivities, and basic to the quality of humanity was the ability to accord each other respect and to recognize the needs of those with whom one came into contact. In 1451, just after the birth of her child, she found that her husband refused to speak to her. Careful to retain her posture of wifely deference towards her husband, she blames his mother for Lichtenštejn's alienation, writing 'And this disgraceful mother, who may not even be human, how much evil she does to me!' (Letter 19). Her maid, Šiermarka, with whom Perchta had discussed her husband's and her in-laws' shortcomings, did not hesitate to exclude Lichtenštejn from the ranks of humanity. After describing his brutal treatment of Perchta and his mother's nastiness, she writes, 'perhaps this person and this old woman are not even human' (Letter 18). Šiermarka underlines her attack on Lichtenštejn's humanity by drawing attention to courtly culture's judgment of peasants as living lives of bestiality when she points out that even a peasant woman expects better treatment from her husband.[29] When the moral quality of humanity was lacking, it was missing in both sexes. In 1463, explaining why she had to leave her husband, Perchta writes to her brothers John and Jošt that when they knew the reason, they would see that the real issue was respect: 'And once you know it, may God grant, you will understand it, that I am striving for nothing else but respect' (Letters 39 Postscript and 40).

Perchta perhaps best illustrated her self-confidence and ability when she took action to safeguard her and her husband's security in 1463, and, in her decision in late 1464 to leave her husband. In rescuing Lichtenštejn from his financial entanglements with his brothers, Perchta exercised her independent legal capacities, mortgaging assets and making contracts. She showed little sign of a wife under her husband's tutelage in 1463 when, free and mobile, she rode from village to village pawning her jewels for cash to redeem her husband's property from lien, and thereby her own dowry (Letters 39 and 40). Two years later she negotiated her peaceful departure from the household of her husband, with provision for the regular payment of her dowry from his estate. Perchta was not active

---

[29] Georges Duby, 'The Courtly Model', in *A History of Women in the West*, II. *Silences of the Middle Ages*, ed. Christine Klapisch-Zuber (Cambridge MA: Harvard University Press, 1992), p. 256.

in the market economy, but she separated her assets from those of her husband and independently brokered deals as did the women of Leiden and Cologne who through such business activities, according to Martha Howell, gained extraordinary prestige and authority and undermined the patriarchal household.[30]

Throughout her life Perchta never ceased agitating for her rights as a Rožmberk and a woman. Even when she adapted to her lot as the unloved wife, she remained the daughter, sister, and aunt imploring her kin to take an interest in her circumstances. She continued her personal supervision of her dowry and her material security. After her move to Vienna, she again had to seek her kin's help in looking after her rights and incomes. The more restrained tone of the later letters to her nephew Henry indicates that she may no longer have expected happiness in her marriage, but she remained determined to receive the income due to her. The rapport she had enjoyed with her father and brothers was missing in her relationship with her nephew. But she continued to take responsibility for herself. In October 1473, after her husband had died, she wrote to an official of her family castle, asking what rights Czech custom gave her regarding her bridewain (Letter 61). She instructed him to send the dowry contract so that she could examine it for herself. On Christmas Day 1474 she wrote her brother-in-law a frosty but polite letter reminding him that he was in arrears in sending her widow's dowry income (Letter 67). She writes her nephew asking him to follow her directions (Letter 68), but, judging from the correspondence, had little success in getting him to act energetically.

Perchta's sense of herself as a person with dignity was related to the conviction which many other medieval women shared: even though they accepted a social position defined as inferior, they proceeded to act as a person who shared or participated in humanity with males. There is no evidence that Perchta saw birth-rights in any sense as natural human rights for all people. She thought of herself as a member of a noble family with all the honor and attributes belonging to that estate. Her appeal to the rights a father owes his child elevated and promoted her natural (*nata*) status over that of her social status; her existence ordained by nature or birth took precedence over her being as a wife defined by social and cultural norms. The issue for her was no less than human respect, and Perchta

---

[30] Martha C. Howell, *Women, Production, and Patriarchy in Late Medieval Cities* (Chicago: University of Chicago Press, 1986), pp. 19–21.

expected to be treated with a basic dignity belonging to people regardless of their sex.

Perchta faced significant obstacles in trying to communicate with her family. Her success resulted from a strategy that depended on cooperation with her servants and kin. As Karen Scott has pointed out, lack of a formal education was not an obstacle for a fourteenth-century woman (such as Catherine of Siena for example) attempting to access the public sphere. Letters were easily dictated, and the oral culture in which a woman such as Perchta was at home may have sharpened her speech and helped her formulate her opinions in a blunt and passionate manner. We cannot conclude, however, as Scott does, that such letters could not be stopped.[31] Simply because some women were able to get their letters through to the intended readers, as Perchta did, does not mean that there were not many who failed. There were enough risks and obstacles that the letters of a woman at odds with the lord of her castle, whether her husband or father-in-law, had to overcome before her words got through to her kin. As the jurist Kornel of Všehrd explained the law at the end of the fifteenth century, a wife was the captive of her husband, and as such her rights to inform and be informed could be severely circumscribed. If a woman was able to write in her own hand, as was Amilie von Pfalz-Zweibrücken-Veldenz, she crafted her letters in secret, excusing her poor script by explaining that she wrote from a soft bed or by a window.[32] The fact that Perchta did not write her own letters even when Henry, her secretary, was gone, suggests that she lacked the ability to do so, but it does not prove it conclusively. She may have been self-conscious about the quality of her handwriting and feared it was illegible, as did the Marchioness Anna of Brandenburg in 1475.[33] Even if a woman could not write, having a faithful secretary and helpful friends and servants made it possible to communicate with the outside world.

Perchta's life lends considerable credence to Howard Bloch's conjecture that courtly poetry's description of aristocratic wives held incommunicado behind their husbands' castle walls reflected the reality of arranged marriages.[34] Women's voices of lament and

---

[31]   Scott, Karen, ' *"Io Catarine"*: Ecclesiastical Politics and Oral Culture in the Letters of Catherine of Siena', in Cherewatuk and Wiethaus, p. 106.

[32]   Nolte, '*Pey eytler finster*', pp. 178–80.

[33]   Nolte, '*Pey eytler finster*', note 23.

[34]   Howard R. Bloch, *Medieval Misogyny and the Invention of Western Romantic Love* (Chicago: University of Chicago Press, 1991), pp. 169–72, and D. Régnier-Bohler, 'Imagining The Self – Exploring Literature', in *Revelations of the Medieval World*, vol. 2, *A History of Private Life*, ed. Duby and Ariès, p. 344.

rage never penetrated beyond those ramparts and never received an answer. In Perchta's case, favorable circumstances and her own determination helped her to be heard. Ulrich of Rožmberk may not always have liked what his daughter wrote. But it was he who provided her with a secretary, indicating that he was prepared to have his daughter express herself even if her messages were troublesome.

As a woman trained for silence, Perchta had to develop a plan of action which included concessions to humility and deference while at the same time pursuing the goal of improving her living conditions.[35] She knew that her first challenge was simply to get her letters beyond the walls of the castle which she shared with her husband and in-laws. Her November 1450 letter to her brother Henry refers to the dangers of communicating: 'unfortunately I have learned something which it is definitely not good for one to publicize or to write about; … it may concern my life' (Letter 11 Postscript). In a postscript she tells the messenger not to inform anyone that he came from her. She tells her brother, the recipient of the letter, that only he should answer the letter, and he should do so in his own hand, and to let her know exactly which day the letter had arrived. On 31 December 1450, she stresses to her father the importance of keeping her letters secret (Letter 16 Postscript). Her father also believed her to be at risk and, it seems, had someone covertly keeping an eye out for her welfare, as she states in the postscript to the same letter. Those that cooperated with Perchta endangered their positions, as one of her husband's servants found out after Perchta's mother-in-law learned that he had delivered a letter to Perchta's father.

Perchta also faced resistance from her kin to her message that her marriage had failed. Her letter in July 1450 to her brother Henry shows this: 'you write to me that I should now stop all writing and messages' (Letter 10). Despite her success at getting her letters to her kin, it seemed to Perchta that her voice was vainly shouting into the wind. On 22 November 1450 she writes to her father, 'Deserted, I have written [my] brother and have often sent messages requesting that he take them to Your Grace; I do not know if he has done this, for my messages have brought me no assistance' (Letter 13). A month later she repeated her request for help, accusing her father of having forgotten about her as though

---

[35] For epistolary strategies in general, see Cherewatuk and Wiethaus, pp. 3–5.

she had never existed. But her words were bearing fruit. Less than a month later her brother sent a knight in his employ as a gesture of support. The knight's visit did not, however, result in concrete and material changes in her conditions. On 13 July 1451 she writes to her brother Henry, 'I have written and sent out so much, but it has helped me not at all, except that I had to suffer more' (Letter 17). She then asks for a feather quilt, a pillow, and a small carpet, for her to sit on while riding in her wagon. Even in 1463, nine years after her family began the dowry payments, she felt deserted by her brother as though through all these years her voice had not been heard. Even in the last years of her life, needing to leave Český Krumlov after her brother's death, Perchta's situation remained precarious and she began corresponding again in order to secure her income. Despite periodic successes, she seems to have been obliged to continue to write letters in pursuit of her own material welfare.

Perchta writes much about her loneliness, and her letters do not describe an actual friendship with any person.[36] She tells us of her strong ties to her brothers and to one of her servants, Šiermarka, but spends most of her marriage and the latter part of her life alone. One reason Perchta said little about her friends and her attachment to them, was because the purpose of her writing was to bring about action to transform her living conditions. Although sparse in details about personal attachments, Perchta's letters draw attention to a number of individuals who showed their sympathy for her by acts of kindness and comfort.

Perchta's first encouragement to speak out about her situation came, surprisingly, from a man in whom her husband placed considerable confidence and who was probably his castle governor: a man we know only as Šek. In the first letter to her father, where she launched her cause in the form of a complaint, she writes that she had been reluctant to address him, but that Šek 'advised me against keeping silence' and suggested she ask her father to send his own official to look into the situation (Letter 7). Šek may have been

---

[36] The late medieval nobility understood friendship as a tie between two lineages whose goals were to accumulate and safeguard property and create mutual political good will. Friendship did not mean emotional affection so much as cooperation between two agnate lines. Karl-Heinz Spieß, *Familie und Verwandschaft im deutschen Hochadel des Spätmittelalters* (Stuttgart: Steiner Verlag 1993), pp. 74–77, and Joel T. Rosenthal, 'Aristocratic Marriage and the English Peerage, 1350–1500: Social Institution and Personal Bond', *Journal of Medieval History* 10 (1984), pp. 181–5.

concerned that his lord's actions towards his wife were unwise, but he was also moved to help her by her plight. Structures of power, whether seen as patriarchal and masculine, or as noble lordship, were not so monolithic as to exclude dissent by fellows and peers.

The key players, without whom Perchta would have remained voiceless, were her own retinue, servants and relatives. It must have been plain to Perchta that her noble status did not free her from dependence on persons of lower estate to get her message published. Her secretary Henry was her most important assistant in helping her communicate with her family and she trusted him completely. Perchta expresses how indispensable he was, when writing to her brother in August 1453. 'As long as I have my Henry, I will be able to write to you', she explains (Letter 26 Postscript). He served faithfully as secretary and encouraged her, having seen with his own eyes how desperate her situation was. While her hard-working and loyal servants were with her, she could communicate with her family and hope to improve her life. She considered them friends and kin.

Perchta also had help from a wider circle of servants in getting her voice heard. In her letter to her brother on 13 July 1451 she tells of an informant, presumably in her husband's court but acting in Perchta's interests, who told her that he had heard that his lord, Lichtenštejn, planned to cut off his wife's access to her family by dismissing the Rožmberk servants. This meant, as Perchta writes, 'I might never again be able to send [anything] to my kinsfolk and be able to let them know anything' (Letter 17). One of Perchta's ladies-in-waiting went beyond merely encouraging her mistress, and wrote her own letter in remarkably sharp terms. The maiden Šiermarka admonishes Perchta's brother (her own employer) for his indifference. She expresses her anger, promising him an emotional confrontation the next time she sees him. His indifference to his sister mystifies her, and she chides him saying that even peasant women expect better treatment than Perchta tolerates (Letter 18).

Perchta also relied on long-serving officials who provided a degree of continuity with the past and who could keep her nephew Henry up to date. After Perchta's brother John died and Henry became lord of the Rožmberk estate, in 1472, she faced the task of convincing him to take an interest in her ongoing struggle for access to her incomes. Perchta referred her nephew to seasoned family officials, such as Jarohněv of Úsuší, who could explain her situation. In her letter of 6 May 1473 she asks Henry to seek the counsel of kin and servants, people who remembered that her troubles were serious and not the product of her imagination (Letter 57).

Perchta also took advantage of the gossip of her servants, as well as of local villagers, to buttress her efforts to persuade her kin to act. Her servants, as well as those in her husband's employ, told her about happenings in, and dangers to, her life. In 1453 she heard that the villagers were talking about her as the cause of higher taxes, because the story was that their lord, her husband, had to bear the cost of her undelivered dowry. She heard from an unnamed source about her husband's dislike for her, for his marriage, and for women in general. She heard about many other things he did, which she considered immoral, and about which she refused to write. She reported threats to her life and to her servants. She used reports about danger to her life, about her husband's lifestyle, and about her undeserved bad name which reflected on the Rožmberk family as a whole. She used what people in and outside her household said as leverage to make her case to her family and move them to act (Letters 15, 16, and 24).

Perchta shared and appreciated the world of servants and villagers. Chris Wickham has argued that the subject-matter of the gossip of different social classes, the diverse ways that stories are told, and the various moral spins placed on information are our best guides as to how distinct social groups work and what they find important.[37] However, we can see in Perchta's use of village gossip that on the Lichtenštejn estates it extended beyond social lines as they are often drawn for medieval society. Perchta regarded what the local commoners said about her as serious and useful. It mattered to Perchta what the villagers said, and she knew it meant something to her brothers and father as well. Hence she could use their talk as a tactic to shame her kin into action on her behalf. Her repeating the gossip of villagers and servants indicates that noblewomen, such as Perchta, lived their lives not only in the ambiance of their aristocratic peers but also with their attendants and with villagers. The common folk among her servants and in villages helped Perchta in her need producing a social bond between noblewoman and commoner.

Perchta's strategy to improve her living conditions depended primarily on the reaction of her father and brothers. Her immediate kin were the recipients of her letters, the audience she most wanted

---

[37] Chris Wickham, 'Gossip and Resistance among Medieval Peasantry', *Past and Present* 160 (1998), p. 23.

to reach, although she doubtless knew that the more others learned of her circumstances the more pressure her kin would feel to act. And although her kin shared the blame for her unfulfilled expectations and her gloom, it was not as though they did nothing. Their very existence reminded Lichtenštejn of the limits to his conduct. Both Perchta and her father knew how important kin was to a wife who felt deserted in her husband's territory. Her father, Ulrich, recognized her dependence on her kin in a note to his son Henry at the time of an anticipated meeting in Vienna in 1455. The Rožmberks were to meet with Perchta and her husband to discuss her unhappy marriage. Ulrich urged his son to wait in Vienna to support his sister when she arrived there. He writes 'Wait for her there, for it would be a huge muddle should she not find you there, for she would have no refuge with anyone, in order to bring these matters to a conclusion' (Letter 30). As we saw above on page 16, Perchta's brother John was the most effective of her kin in improving her living conditions, thanks to his willingness to break a long-standing family alliance and to support his father's rival to the throne. Undoubtedly Perchta's indefatigable campaign of letter-writing was an important factor in moving her brother to support George of Poděbrady as king. In exchange Poděbrady canceled a large monetary debt and John of Rožmberk was able to direct the family's funds and deliver Perchta's dowry.

Also important to Perchta were the friends and kin who were her neighbors in Moravia and Upper Austria. Perchta's more distant kin helped her overcome the initial displeasure her brother and father expressed over her writing. Her kinsman George of Kravař served as a nearby conduit communicating her voice to her father and brother. In 1464 he wrote to John of Rožmberk that over the years he had sent her letters on to him, not regretting the expenses or the effort, and now that Perchta's life was in danger John should act (Letters 32, 35, and 43). In Třeboň, the most easterly Rožmberk castle, Anéžka received her sister's letters sent by George, possibly paid the messenger, and sent them on to Český Krumlov. In 1470, when Perchta was on the family estate, Anéžka cared for the sick Perchta and tried to mediate her ongoing concerns (Letters 45 and 51). Even political rivals of her father helped Perchta. Early on, Aleš of Šternberk, a leading baron of the Hussite–Polish party opposed to Rožmberk's Catholic–Austrian party, but with whom Ulrich was in frequent communication on both public and domestic matters, on his own initiative sent Rožmberk a report about Perchta's living conditions based on what he saw (Letter 10).

As important as all her auxiliary channels were, Perchta wanted to describe the circumstances of her life in her own words so as to make the argument most advantageous to her. She relied on the negotiating abilities of her kin, but did not stand by watching helplessly. In her letter to her brother Henry in 1453 she describes her husband's failure to keep a promise to provide for her materially during her pregnancy, and how the local public blamed her for a new tax. She warns her brother against negotiating without consulting her prior to any meeting with her husband's brother. She says her husband would talk a great deal, make meaningless promises, and Perchta feared Henry would be taken in by her brother-in-law's manipulation and would make an agreement not suitable to her. As she expressed it:

> I would be very unhappy about that, ... Therefore, if I see you then, and if I report some things to you, this might change your attitude, and, as it would happen after you hear what I have to say to you, it would be very clear that this [information] comes from me. (Letter 24)

Perchta knew that many of the meetings to discuss her life were closed to her. But she wanted those who spoke on her behalf to know directly from her what her situation was.

Her confidence in her ability to speak for herself was also evident in March 1455. At this time her dowry payments were coming in and she was in her family castle, Český Krumlov. She was concerned about a forthcoming meeting where a trusted family official, John Rús of Čemin, would represent her. She told her brother Henry that she had insisted on her position in discussions with her other brother, and that she had personally told John Rús what she wanted said (Letter 28). She was of course limited by political and social realities which excluded women from the actual meetings where the two parties worked out their differences. Both orally and in writing, she laid out the terms to her kin of how they were to negotiate her interests. In the same way, at her husband's death, she immediately acted to get a copy of her dowry in her hands because she knew his kin would renew their efforts to take over her incomes and property. Although she continued her deferential pose towards her nephew, she also instructed him as to his course of action. As she expressed it in December 1474, 'Now I have ordered this Martin [Tulmacz] to let you know all about what I think [and] I ask you, all my dear kinsmen, that you will allow me to direct you in all this' (Letter 68). Her dependence on her male kin circumscribed the possibilities for action, but within this context she expressed herself clearly and strongly, reflecting the sense of a person born into the Rožmberk family. As she once reminded her brother Henry, it was from him that she had learned how to speak in her own interest (Letter 10).

Perchta succeeded in conveying her concerns and wishes to her father and brothers with the help of many parties. She began with her own strong sense of self, with her feeling that her disappointment and sadness were important and that others should know about them and have an interest in them. People within her immediate surroundings participated in the project, encouraging her to speak, writing down her words, adding their own words to hers, and protecting and carrying her letters to their intended recipients. In the end the letters reached their destination and partially accomplished her goals. Perchta's situation improved, even if only a little. She obtained her dowry, and a somewhat better relationship with her husband for a few months. When faced with new threats from her husband's kin, she got her husband's and her brothers' consent to leave her marital home and to return to the home of her childhood, with promises of a regular income. Although she feared for her life during her marriage, in fact she outlived her husband. In August 1473, at the age of forty-four, she writes, 'I am letting you know that my lord and husband has unfortunately been brought down by death, may God be merciful to him' (Letter 58). She then proceeds to ask for a copy of her dowry letter. Her letter informs its readers of her husband's death in sober and moderate terms, Perchta being aware that it is she who is announcing his death, not he hers. She was still alive to fight on her own behalf against threats from her in-laws.

Perchta's training was supposed to construct a gender identity along lines of obedience, silence, and submission, but she was also taught to think of herself with pride and dignity as a member of a great family. Aristocratic women had to create some kind of coherence and continuity in their minds out of two contradictory lines of upbringing. The experience of Anéžka and Perchta, and the support they received from father, brothers, and friendly aristocrats, suggests that the teaching that regulated norms for medieval femininity and the practices to enforce them were not rigid. Females' identities were molded along lines of obedience, but when they rejected conformity to the dominant norms their personhood was not called into question, nor did their lives and identities as women become incoherent or unintelligible. Perchta's relationship to her brother John shows that women and men had the resilience to adapt to needs that required alternative patterns of gender behavior.

Perchta's coping with the dissonance between accepted social conventions of female inferiority and her sense of human dignity fit in with the experience of other medieval women who expressed themselves in letters. They accepted a definition of themselves as inferior, but then proceeded to subvert the notion of secondary status. By implicitly restricting inferiority to social and cultural roles, women claimed that they were part of the human race by nature essentially on a par with males. To survive and to be effective they proclaimed themselves weak, dependent, and submissive. However, there were women who, when they had something to say or do, appealed to their status as human beings and took action.

Do we then hear a female voice in Perchta's correspondence when the larger script was written by men? Luce Irigaray, Judith Butler, and others have argued that civilization has been so completely suffused with the male principle that the feminine has been erased and is invisible.[38] Philosophical, political, moral, and legal discourse has been monopolized by the male perspective which sees itself as active and the female as passive. The female sex is not a sex in this cultural discourse. Such a scenario in many ways describes late medieval Europe. The system of marriages which entangled Perchta was almost entirely organized by a father or a brother who chose the spouse for his daughter or sister.

However, medieval Bohemian society also reflected considerable unease over a structure of marriage in which women were denied freedom to choose. This discomfort was reflected in Czech popular culture. One saying went 'Is there any bride as unhappy as I, wed as I am to a stranger?' Vlasta, the leader of the maidens' war against the men, described in the founding legend of the Czech people, urged on her followers with the promise that if they won the war, 'we will choose our own husbands, and we will beat them when we wish'.[39] Her words reflected both male anxieties as well as women's anger. Such undertones of female rebellion can be seen in actual marriages.[40] Nevertheless, for women, the method of forming

---

[38] Luce Irigaray, *This Sex Which is not One*, and Butler, *Bodies that Matter*, pp. 33–53.

[39] Igor Němec et al., *Slova a dějiny* [Words and History] (Prague: Academia, 1980), p. 39, and Jiří Daňhelka et al., *Staročeské kronika tak řečeného Dalimila* [The Old Czech Chronicle of the So-called Dalimil], 1 (Prague: Academia, 1988), p. 219.

[40] John M. Klassen, *Warring Maidens, Captive Wives and Hussite Queens,* East European Monographs no. 527 (New York: Columbia University Press, 1999), pp. 1–3 and 103–04.

marriages generally remained part of a burdensome and unfair social system.

The challenge of finding the authentic voice of a person applies not only to women, because both sexes can live in confining and onerous circumstances. There were also males in late medieval Europe who were unhappy with the social and cultural situation and who offered solutions for change. One male critic of medieval society was Perchta's fellow-countryman Peter Chelčický who died in the early 1460s. He was a member of the lesser nobility who, after the death of John Hus, dedicated himself to preaching about the Christian life. Chelčický fundamentally criticized the male-constructed system of war, the coercive three-tiered class structure, and the privileged status of men. As a relatively favored male, Chelčický was more of an observer than a participant in misery. Still, his writings stand as an example of a male who censured an imperfect society and a Church in need of reform, and whose ideas were admired by his contemporaries even if they did not often act on them.[41]

Perchta would rather not have been married to Lichtenštejn. Had she been given a choice, she would have preferred to write about a life of independence or of times spent with a husband who was her companion and friend. Who knows what she would have dictated to her secretary Henry had she made her own marriage? But given the faulty system in which Perchta found herself, she uttered her concerns eloquently, persistently, and, to a degree, effectively. She rejected her father's priorities and his choice of husband for her. She used her own words to persuade her father and her brother to reconsider, and to take action on her behalf. Finding herself in an unhappy position, Perchta undauntedly pursued her welfare, her dignity, and life itself. Perchta's fame was such that in later centuries she became identified as the legendary 'white lady'.

Many European cultures possess fables about white ladies, spirits, or ghosts, doomed to wander because they had no peace, and who appeared to people by day and by night. In some countries they surfaced in black when foretelling bad news and in white when coming with good news.[42] Most of what we know about these ghosts

---

[41] Howard Kaminsky, 'Peter Chelčický: Treatises on Christianity and the Social Order', *Studies in Medieval and Renaissance History* 1 (1964), pp. 107–77, and Klassen, *Warring Maidens*, pp. 167–73.

[42] Frank Wollman, 'Pověst o bílé paní v literatuře a v tradicích českého lidu' [The Legend about the White Lady in the Literature and Traditions of the Czech People], *Národopisný věstník českoslovanský* 7 (1913), p. 183.

has been filtered through the eyes of seventeenth-century Jesuits or nineteenth-century Romantic nationalists with their own agendas, so we cannot say for certain how popular culture first envisioned them.[43] In the Czech versions the white lady is connected with pre-Christian beliefs about female apparitions who possessed supernatural powers, and who benignly supervised the transition into life at birth and from life at death. They walked the fields, appeared at wells, and in winter visited places of family activity and life such as wash-houses. Some of these white ladies concentrated their efforts on protecting children. The white lady was the ruler of winter, whose efforts were especially welcome during the shortest and coldest days of the year. According to František Dvorský, the common people of Bohemia sometimes named them after the renowned ruling and warring women, Libuše, Vlasta, and Šarka, figures in the founding legend of their nation.[44]

At some point between her death and the mid-seventeenth century, the common people of south Bohemia began to associate Perchta of Rožmberk with the white lady and her acts of kindness. By the seventeenth century Perchta became identified with two separate Czech legends about a white lady: in one she comforted babies in distress and in the second she supervised the feeding of the hungry. In 1539, the white lady brought her benevolent presence to the Rožmberk household when she entered the bedroom of the infant Peter Vok of Rožmberk, soothing the fretting child back to sleep. Sometimes she was described with a cheerful face, with braided hair adorned in a wreath, or loose and curly. To some she appeared with saddened eyes, in a white widow's dress decorated with white streamers. She walked through the house as though at home, with key in hand as though she had some business of the castle to look after. If someone greeted her she responded politely, her voice like a soft breeze. The legend about the white lady who fed the poor was important to the south Bohemian lords of Jindřichův Hradec, a branch related to the Rožmberks. Since the fifteenth century it had been the custom for the lords of Hradec to provide money once a year for a meal of crushed or ground grain boiled in sweetened water or milk, in amounts that fed anywhere from 3,000 to 8,000 people. In 1659, the Jesuit, Jan Tanner, identified the white

---

[43] Peter Mat'a, 'Zrození Tradice' [The Birth of a Tradition], *Opera Historica* 6 (1998), pp. 538–46.

[44] Dvorský, *Perchta*, pp. 132–38.

lady as the protector of the tradition of the annual distribution of this sweet porridge.

The memory of Perchta of Rožmberk obviously played an important and positive role in popular memory, because, with the coming of the Counter-Reformation in the seventeenth-century, the Jesuits saw her potential and recruited her as an ally for their cause. Jesuit interest in her as a champion of reformed Catholicism reflected her popularity in the common mind, as well as her importance to the powerful local nobility. The ghost of Perchta had apparently learned Latin and helped the pro-Habsburg forces drive the Swedes out of the country. The Jesuits put her story into writing for the first time, and their account influenced all later versions.[45] Thus, Perchta of Rožmberk, the woman who recounted her sorrow by letter in the fifteenth century, became identified in the popular mind as one qualified through her suffering to address the misery of others.

[45] Mat'a, 'Zrození Tradice', p. 546.

Select Bibliography

Archival and printed sources

Archív Český čili Staré písemné památky české a moravské [The Czech archives or ancient written Bohemian and Moravian documents], vol. 4, ed. Franišek Palacký (Prague: Kronberger a Řivnáč, 1844)

Archív Český čili Staré písemné památky české a moravské [The Czech archives or ancient written Bohemian and Moravian documents], vol. 11, ed. Josef Kalousek (Prague: Bursík & Kohout, 1892) [Contains the Czech letters of Perchta of Rožmberk]

Listář a listinář Oldřicha z Rožmberka 1418–1462 [Letters and Documents of Ulrich of Rožmberk 1418–1462], vols. 1–3, ed. Blažena Rynešová (Prague: Státní Tiskárna, 1929), vol. 4, ed. Blažena Rynešová and Josef Pelikan (Prague: Statní pedagogické nakladatelství, 1954)

Sedláček, August, 'Anéžka z Rožmberka', *Sborník Historický na oslavu desítí letého trvaní 'Klubu historického' v Praze* (Prague, 1883) [Contains the letters of Anéžka of Rožmberk]

Státní Oblastní Archív in Třeboň, [SOA], *Z Cizí Rodi z Líchtenstejn*

Tomaš Štítný, *Knížky o hře šachové a jiné* [Thomas Štítný. Books about the Game of Chess and other things], František Šimek, and Miloslav Kaňak, eds (Prague: Státní Nakladatelství Krásné Literatury, Hudby a Umění, 1956)

Selected Secondary Sources

Ahlgren, Gillian T. W., 'Visions and Rhetorical Strategy in the Letters of Hildegard of Bingen', in *Dear Sister: Medieval Women and the Epistolary Tradition*, ed. Karen Cherewatuk and Ulrike Wiethaus (Philadelphia: University of Pennsylvania Press, 1993), pp. 46–63

Amt, Emilie, ed., *Women's Lives in Medieval Europe* (London: Routledge, 1993)

Bloch, Howard R., *Medieval Misogyny and the Invention of Western Romantic Love* (Chicago: University of Chicago Press, 1991)

Braunstein, Philip, 'The Emergence of the Individual: Toward Intimacy. The Fourteenth and Fifteenth Centuries', *Revelations of the Medieval World*, ed. Georges Duby and Philippe Ariès, vol. 2, *A*

History of Private Life (Cambridge MA: Harvard University Press, 1988), pp. 507–632

Butler, Judith *Gender Trouble. Feminism and the Subversion of Identity* (New York: Routledge, 1990)

Bynum, Carolyn W., *Jesus as Mother: Studies in the Spirituality of the High Middle Ages* (Berkeley: University of California Press, 1982)

Cherewatuk, Karen, 'Radegund and Epistolary Tradition', in Cherewatuk and Wiethaus, pp. 20–45

Cherewatuk, Karen, and Wiethaus, Ulrike, eds, *Dear Sister: Medieval Women and the Epistolary Tradition* (Philadelphia: University of Pennsylvania Press, 1993)

Classen, Albrecht, 'Female Epistolary Literature from Antiquity to the Present: An Introduction', *Studia Neophilologica* 60 (1988), pp. 3–13.

Duby, Georges, 'The Courtly Model', in *A History of Women in the West*, II, *Silences of the Middle Ages,* ed. Christiane Klapisch-Zuber (Cambridge MA: Harvard University Press, 1992), pp. 250–66

Duby, Georges, *The Knight, the Lady, and the Priest: The Making of Modern Marriage in Medieval France* (Chicago: University of Chicago Press, 1993)

Duggan, Anne, ed., *Queens and Queenship in Medieval Europe* (Woodbridge: Boydell Press, 1997)

Gladden, Samuel L., 'Hildegard's Awakening: A Self-Portrait of Disruptive Excess', in *Representations of the Feminine in the Middle Ages*, ed. Bonnie Wheeler (Cambridge: Academia Press, 1993), pp. 217–34

Grundmann, Herbert, *Religiöse Bewegungen im Mittelalter* (Hildesheim: G. Olm, 1970)

Heymann, Frederick, G., *George of Bohemia: King of the Heretics* (Princeton: Princeton University Press, 1965)

Hufton, Olwen, *The Prospect before Her: A History of Women in Western Europe, 1500–1800* (New York: HarperCollins, 1996)

Irigaray, Luce, *This Sex Which is not One*, trans. Catherine Porter (Ithaca: Cornell University Press, 1985)

Kaminsky, Howard, *A History of the Hussite Revolution* (Berkeley: University of California Press, 1967)

Kaminsky, Howard, 'Peter Chelčický: Treatises on Christianity and the Social Order', *Studies in Medieval and Renaissance History* 1 (1964), pp. 105–79

Kaminsky, Howard, 'The Problematics of Later Medieval Heresy', in *Husitství, Reformace, Renesance*, I [Hussitism, Reformation, Renaissance], ed. Jaroslav Pánek et al. (Prague: Historical Institute, 1994), pp. 133–56

Kiple, Kenneth, ed., *The Cambridge World History of Human Disease* (Cambridge: Cambridge University Press, 1993)

Kirshner, Julius, 'Wives' Claims against Insolvent Husbands in Late Medieval Italy', in *Women in the Medieval World*, ed. Julius Kirshner and Suzanne Wemple (Oxford: Oxford University Press, 1985), pp. 256–302

Klassen, John, 'Gifts for the Soul and Social Charity in Late Medieval Bohemia', *Materielle Kultur und Religiöse Stiftung im Spätmittelalter. Veröffentlichungen des Instituts für Mittelalterliche Realkunde Österreichs* Nr. 12 (Vienna, 1990), pp. 63–81

Klassen, John. M., *The Nobility and the Making of the Hussite Revolution*, East European Monographs, vol. 47 (New York: Columbia University Press, 1978)

Klassen, John M., *Warring Maidens, Captive Wives and Hussite Queens,* East European Monographs no. 527 (New York: Columbia University Press, 1999)

Martin, Paula, 'A Brightness of Purple Lightening: Hildegard of Bingen's Self-Perception', in *Representations of the Feminine in the Middle Ages*, ed. Bonnie Wheeler (Cambridge: Academia Press, 1993), pp. 235–46

Moriarty, Catherine, ed., *The Voice of the Middle Ages in Personal Letters. 1100–1500* (New York: Peter Bedrick Books, 1989)

Nolte, Cordula, *'Pey eytler finster in einem weichen pet geschrieben.* Eigenhändige Briefe in der Familienkorrespondenz der Markgrafen von Brandenburg (1470–1530)', in *Adelige Welt und familiäre Beziehung,* ed. Heinz-Dieter Heimann (Potsdam: Verlag für Berlin-Brandenburg, 2000), pp. 177–202

Parsons, John C., ed., *Medieval Queenship* (New York: St. Martin's Press, 1993)

Polívka, Miloslav, 'A Contribution to the Problem of Property Differentiation of the Lesser Nobility in the Pre-Hussite Period in Bohemia', *Economic History* 2 (1978), pp. 331–59

Polívka, Miloslav, 'Ulrich von Rosenberg und seine Umgebung', in *Adelige Welt und familiäre Beziehung*, ed. Heinz-Dieter Heimann (Potsdam: Verlag für Berlin-Brandenburg, 2000), pp. 59–72

Régnier-Bohler, D., 'Imagining the Self-Exploring Literature', *Revelations of the Medieval World*, ed. George Duby and Philippe Ariès, vol. 2, *A History of Private Life* (Cambridge, MA: Harvard University Press, 1988), pp. 311–94

Richards, Earl, ' "Seulette a part". The "Little Woman on the Sidelines" Takes up her Pen: The Letters of Christine de Pizan', in Cherewatuk and Wiethaus, pp. 139–70

Rosenthal, Joel. T., 'Aristocratic Marriage and the English Peerage, 1350–1500: Social Institution and Personal Bond', *Journal of Medieval History* 10 (1984), pp. 181–93

Scott, Karen, ' "*Io Catarine*": Ecclesiastical Politics and Oral Culture in the Letters of Catherine of Siena', in Cherewatuk and Wiethaus, pp. 87–121

Spieß, Karl-Heinz, *Familie und Verwandschaft im deutschen Hochadel des Spätmittelalters* (Stuttgart: Steiner Verlag, 1993)

Strauss Gerhard, ed., *Manifestations of Discontent in Germany on the Eve of the Reformation* (Bloomington: University of Indiana Press, 1971)

Stuard, Susan M., *A State of Deference: Ragusa/Dubrovnik in the Medieval Centuries* (Philadelphia: University of Pennsylvania Press, 1992)

Thomas, Alfred, *Anne's Bohemia: Czech Literature and Society, 1310–1420* (Minneapolis MN: University of Minnesota Press, 1998)

Tierney, Brian, *The Rights of Natural Law: Studies on Natural Rights, Natural Law and Church Law 1150–1625*, no. 5 of Emory University Studies in Law and Religion (Atlanta GA: Scholars Press, 1997)

Walsh, Katherine, 'Verkaufte Töchter? Überlegungen zu Aufgabenstellung und Selbstvertgefühl von in die Ferne verheirateten Frauen anhand ihrer Korrespondenz', *Jahrbuch des Vorarlberger Landesmuseumsvereins* 135 (1991), pp. 129–44

Watt, Diane ' "No Writing for Writing's Sake": The Language of Service and Household Rhetoric in the Letters of the Paston Women', in Cherewatuk and Wiethaus, pp. 122–138

Wickham, Chris, 'Gossip and Resistance among Medieval Peasantry', *Past and Present* 160 (1998), pp. 3–24

Wiethaus, Ulrike, ' "If I had an Iron Body": Maria de Hout', in Cherewatuk and Wiethaus, pp. 171–91

Wunder, Heidi, *He is the Sun, She is the Moon: Women in Early Modern Germany* (Cambridge MA: Harvard University Press, 1998)

Index